Praise for Lola's Walkabout

Lola's Walkabout is a terrific and thoroughly engaging story of a young woman and her journey from an awkward and confused teenager to a moment of self-discovery and empowerment. In her late teens Lola swims in a sea of despair and hope as she faces bullying from her peers. But as the story progresses Lola learns to own both despair and hope and the awkward power of being female. It is a compelling work which deals with complex human experience in a manner that brings the black and white issue to the surface. The narrative jumps out of the pages with its sensuous descriptions of the Australian landscape, strong dialogue and characters. An honest piece of writing for any age.

ELLA FILAR, playwright, and drama and cabaret performer

Lola's Walkabout is an easy read about a coming of age story in modern day Australia that has some surprising twists that will have you not wanting to put the book down. Lola's voice is one that is not heard in Australian fiction today and one that needs to be heard more. This book would particularly appeal to teenagers who are different and feel they don't fit in. Inspiring and courageous, Lola's example of overcoming her own fears and societal constraints and striking out on her own path will not only move you but challenge you to take a fresh look at yourself and society.

ANGEL MISHAS, transpersonal counsellor

Lola's walkabout

MARISA RITA ZAMMIT

First published in 2016
by Marisa Rita Zammit

Copyright © Marisa Rita Zammit 2016

The moral right of the author has been asserted.
All rights reserved. No part of this publication may be reproduced or transmitted by any person or entity (including Google, Amazon or similar organisations), in any form or means, electronic or mechanical, including photocopying, recording, scanning or by any information storage and retrieval system without prior permission in writing from the author.

National Library of Australia
Cataloguing-in-Publication data:

Zammit, Marisa Rita, author.
Lola's Walkabout / Marisa Rita Zammit.

ISBN: 978-0-994-6221-05 (paperback)

For young adults.
Cultural pluralism — Juvenile fiction.
Aboriginal Australians — Juvenile fiction.
Young adult fiction.
Alice Springs (N.T.) — Juvenile fiction.
Melbourne (Vic.) — Juvenile fiction.

A823.4

Cover design and typesetting by Ilura Design
www.ilurapress.com

Printed and bound by Ingram Spark Australia

To Kai, Lex, and Ange

Contents

Chapter One

the nightclub	9
the meeting	16
the date	24
at home	34
paris	40
somewhere else	45
the invasion	55

Chapter Two

second chance	117
sex and the goth … and … what did really happen that night?	119
looking for jasmin	148

Chapter Three

rapture in the desert	171
Acknowledgements	204
About the Author	205

Chapter One

the nightclub

It wasn't about getting to know someone, it was more about a certain style. It was about swimming in the trance music with the beat of edginess, diving into an exploration sustained by an image that would always be adhered to. Never running into pointlessness. But then pointlessness had become an image. Being like this could be fun and adventurous. Paris and Jasmin held fascination over every testosterone stick in the market that roared near their cult of fun. But the dark beat of the nightclub would ravage their days.

The beat, reduced to a repetitive thump outside the bathroom, gave Lola an empty feeling. The floor cold with slimy coating saluting alcohol and decadence. Raspy voiced women complaining to their friends in the next dunny about having to smoke outside the club, as they finished and flushed. Toilet paper squandering like a parachute falling dead on its tracks covering the walls. Yeah, let's get out of here, some would say. It was cool to be thrown into the abyss, an empty space outside of everything, you left alone with the rigors of sex, drugs and alcohol, there an image of yourself outside of your upbringing, somewhere lost to find yourself. Being incoherent something perfectly coherent.

You'd know that part of the image was that just being a nice person was old-fashioned and grungy cool was higher in the life stakes. Being a virgin was certainly an embarrassment. Lola was a virgin. Lola was cautious. And Lola was confused. Were her friends just a bit too plucky with their self-adornment? Were they immoral in their amorality? Were they also selfish? Was Lola's path to self-discovery aligned with theirs? Was experimentation with everything an obstacle or a way to freedom?

'Bitch, bitch!' Jasmin laughed. Her talons were slashers, but well preserved. Not poking anyone in the eye during a sexual escapade would be a miracle. Ha, sexual religiosity … Lola would try to appreciate the aesthetics of her friends' ritual entries into womanhood. But what about her own?

Her tart-dirt friends would act like animals ravaging a mirror with lipstick.

Their image would reflect back 'desirable' as they would fixed the curve of the lash one more time with a tinge of more mascara, and fill their lips a bit more for pink luminosity in a nightclub. Then breath and fingerprints smudged on glass like chocolate. And it goes back to mothball grandma rooms with old age ridiculed by lipstick festooning with words like OLD BITCH. Granddaughters surreptitiously smoking in pleasant sun rooms that escape into timeless nature. With all the grubby angst of their time, they'd act to get spanked.

Lola would watch these 'bad girls', feeling like an outsider, a drag but curious, and finally—confused! Dressed in black, while they dressed in tart's latest for a dieted body. Food diet was the only discipline they had. What happened to her friends? Suddenly, they were hit in the face with their own hormones, and this made them lurid and self-centred. Lola was hit in the face with her hormones, too. But how would they express in her?

'Are you real!' Jasmin shouted, leaning back on the brown tiled wall, 'You broke my nail when you grabbed me!'

'When did I grab you?' Paris warped her face in front of the mirror, sliding into an erotic object of derision, as she poked her tongue and wobbled her new piercing.

Sober Lola felt dull. Her low, internal voice suppressed by their external extravagance, her clothing dark, obscure, streamlined. She pressed against the wall as women opened the door to get out of the bathroom. She couldn't wait to get out of its enclosure that smelt of trashy perfume and repugnant 'girlishness'.

Outside, figures moved against zappy hallucinogenic lights, bodies then pumping with sweat and relieved with air conditioning, and fans caressing and cooling the skin, but only momentarily. The bodies mechanistically frenzied inside a trance beat.

Hours went past.

'Let's get out of here!' screamed Paris.

'Now?' Jasmin jutted her head towards Paris as she shook inside the tremor.

'They're waiting, they're gonna get trashed before we get there!' Paris stayed still and held Jasmin's bracelet, and pleaded with her. 'We've been here long enough!'

Lola looked forward to the fresh air, but then it was a case of everything the boys were doing.

Crisp morning air outside the nightclub. Lola looked at her mobile, it was four am. The nightclub's crescendo was waning to a still. People emerging out of its cave like bug-eyed zombies.

The boys came out from the upmarket pub across the road, tight pants, gelled hair, shiny shoes and a kick in their walk as they pranced to the beat flaring out of the cars going past.

'Hey, I got some ees.' Sam's hand shook inside his pant's pocket.

'Quiet, fuckwit.' Tony pulled Sam's immaculate shirt. There had been an outbreak of drug use, and security standing by the entrance of the nightclub had been briefed by the police. And a watch on binge drinking. 'Let's get out of here!' Tony warned.

Lola felt numb to the taking of the drug. Even worse, concern to being an accomplice would have been seen as too responsible and boring. Paris and Jasmin were always interested, animated and involved, but Lola was never going to be fully integrated.

In Sam's car, the fresh air rushed from the window, and the scenery shift was a distraction against the giggling voices of Paris and Jasmin as they reclined in the back seat, their legs splayed, taking major room. Paris was holding the cachet. Lola, face by the window, was enjoying the dawn, the first morning of autumn.

Suddenly, Tony turned the radio on and Kesha ambushed the car with her Tik Tok. The boys drove through South Yarra heading to the city. People insinuating their presence in the streets looked refreshed and tickled by Kesha's bubble-gum clamour about pick me ups, partying, and bust ups.

'Hey, you. Come here!' A guy chased the car, his arms flailing in a drunken stupor.

Lola made a decision. 'Can you take me home?'

'You're a party-pooper Lola.' Sam moved his head slightly away from the wheel to look down at Lola.

'I'm just really … I don't know, tired I guess …'

'OK.' Sam scrunched a chuckle in his throat. 'Lola, you're one hot chick, especially in that long black dress. You look like some kind of intellectual, feminist mann. Girls teach her how to dress more the tart.'

'Get lost, what tart!' Jasmin cracked up.

'It's real, isn't it? That's what you are?' Sam pressed down on the pedal.

Jasmin smiled. 'Lola looks like an emo or a lezzo.'

Those snide remarks again.

There it was, the only weatherboard house in Toorak, built by migrants, expressing earnest hard work and sacrifice, and flanked by bigger houses.

Lola got out of the car. 'Bye.' She flicked her hand across her face as if to shoo away a fly.

Sam's head popped out of the window. 'You're missing out. Don't forget this!' He threw her fake ID at her. Paris and Jasmin stuck their tongues out, perhaps in jest, but perhaps also, in disrespect. The Besties drove off.

the meeting

A few midnights later Lola found herself standing in front of the brass rimmed door of Paris' two-story house. She hesitated as she placed her finger on the buzzer, acknowledging she was annoyed at herself for being there. But Paris phoned. And Paris meant business. Paris opened the door slowly, and she seemed to be sliding against the edge of it, 'I'm glad you're here.' She exhaled the smoke from her joint. She was dressed in a blue satin, low décolletage gown.

'Why do you want me here?' Lola coughed.

'I've met someone special.' She exhaled, this time aiming towards the manicured garden.

'Who?'

'Come inside.'

The lounge room trembled with candle light making the softly furnished space very shadowy. Her parents were gone for a few weeks for a wedding ceremony.

Paris flopped her hand forward, 'Sitting before us is …' Paris paused. Then continued. 'I don't know …' Paris played with her hair and smiled. She waited for an acknowledging look from the man. 'What's your name sweetheart?' She pouted. No response. 'He does not ANSWER!' she said turning to Lola. A young man who looked Aboriginal sat a seat away from Jasmin. He was dressed in a yellow T-shirt and blue jeans. His eyes, dark skin and full lips pulsating in front of a candle light.

'He was busking in Brunswick Street, playing a guitar like he was playing a woman.' Paris strummed her hand against her belly. Expressive as usual on a joint, she inhaled the smoke, and then exhaled. 'He tuned up even more with me and Jasmin there.' She looked around her, 'Omigod!' She whirled. 'Look at this place, isn't it great with the candles!' Paris' moods were rotating like a kaleidoscope in the wind. Jasmin was red-eyed and out-of-it, wearing a black lingerie with black fish net stockings and stiletto high boots. Almost toppling from the chair, she looked like an incompetent prostitute. Paris snapped into cognition: 'Come on girl, we've got work to do!' Jasmin gave that joker look and re-aligned her seated position. She would stay like that until action would borne itself on this occasion.

Lola stepped towards the young man, a little. 'Hello. What's your name?' He stared back.

'Can he speak English?' Lola whispered to Paris.

'I don't know. He's sooo mys-terrr-iousss. He always looks like he's gonna do us, but … then he doesn't.' Paris twirled her hair again giving a sweet and sour smile at Lola. 'He'd be sooo good in a threesome. Man of few words, all physical. He would really be a … I don't need offend you, so I won't say it.'

Again, a condescending remark. Lola dispelled Paris for a moment and turned her attention to the young man again. The man's eyes were tracking things down. But he was unmoved. He appeared proud. He had the most beautiful eyes that just melted, as the smoke shifted around the room, heavy and effective.

Paris watched the man like she was thinking about something she was going to do. She took a step, looking as nimble as a cat, placed her joint on the tray beside him, and bent down to his level. She hovered her lips gently over his thick lips and strategically pulled back her arms to bring out the cleavage. Movement. He flicked his arm, motioning her away. He stood, strutted to the door, opened it, and walked off. Fresh air belting in.

Lola's heart rose a notch. Paris slumped back on the sofa he was just seated on. 'He must be gay!' She looked at Lola and cocked her brow.

'I'll see you some time Paris.'

Lola knew what she was going to do. And Paris didn't. And that felt so good.

The man was all movement. His long figure walked quickly and furtively in the pale light. Lola could still feel the marijuana smoke inside her throat, but she was refreshed by the air and ran to him. An enthusiasm she hardly ever experienced had warmed itself to her. She remembered his dark eyes and dark skin in the incandescent room, his majestic stance, his inscrutability that twisted itself around him to protect him from exploitation.

'Hello! Hey, please wait!' She remembered he could not speak English.

'Are you OK?'

He stopped. 'Yes.'

'Y–o–u doo sspeak English!' Lola was out of breath.

'Yeah of course I do.' He walked self-assured.

'I think you made them believe that you couldn't.' Lola stayed with his pace.

'I had them on.'

'Why?'

'Why are you so interested?'

'W-e-ll, that doesn't happen to them. M-e-n don't just walk off. No MAN has ever done that.' She stopped, waited, breathed in, and caught up again.

'Pretty capricious, aren't they.' The man turned his face to Lola.

'Yes, how did you know?'

'I taught them a lesson. I've got respect for myself. I'm not some specimen.'

'No, you're not.' Lola paused. 'They shouldn't treat you like that.'

They both stopped. 'Let me ask you something,' he said.

Lola stepped closer towards him. He paused and waited, looked around, and looked at Lola. 'Why do you stay with those girls?'

'I don't know.' There was really no answer there. She had always been with them. She stumbled upon them in primary school, stayed with them. It must have been unconscious, wanting to be seen with the superficial best, mirroring her parents' intention to live in a suburb that was far beyond their income capacity, and each gray hair there to prove it. Was it about not being happy with yourself, not fitting in anywhere? Was it about hanging out with people who make you feel bad about yourself so you don't have to do it? Maybe being happy would be too painful, as that would get you in touch with who you are. Or maybe, in fact, she needed to learn things from them. An almost repugnant thought.

'You don't know? I think you do. I think you know about life much more than them,' he said like he mysteriously knew things.

'Why do you say this?'

'I can tell the way you were acting with them, that you just don't belong there, and that you're much better than them. But you don't think so. No one has ever told you anything good about you, have they?'

'No. Not outside my grandparents and my mum and dad.'

'In a few weeks I'm going to the Northern Territory. I've got good friends there, real friends, and of course my family. Why don't you get out of Melbourne for a while and stay with me?' He spoke urgently like the time they met was really important or it was the beginning or end of something. 'Where do you live?' He stepped even closer to her.

'I live down the block.' His scent was natural and earthy. He was sexy.

The moon was getting paler and paler as the light came in. The clouds frothing up looked like lavender mushrooms in the sky. It seemed like the morning was only for them to see. Autumn leaves from the road rushed to them. The breeze was blowing in their direction.

'I live here.' Lola half pointed to her demure weatherboard house. Then it clicked automatically that this man was different. He couldn't have been into impressions like her friends were. 'What's your phone number?' She felt comfortable enough to assert herself, like never before.

'Got a paper and pen?' He didn't seem to have a mobile. 'My name's Kua, what's yours?'

'Lola.' Lola searched her body. Her pockets were deep, upholding her VCE profile of library cards, scrap papers and pens. Her lack of pink and girlie accoutrements making her feel unfeminine. But then again, Kua didn't choose her friends. Perhaps Kua liked unusual girls? She wondered.

Before she could think any more, she found a paper and pen. She passed it to him. As he wrote down the number he said, 'Ring me.' He gave back the paper and pen and left with hands in pockets and swing to his stride.

At last somebody likes me.

the date

Blue cafe was warm with a fireplace, and decked out with couches. Lola chose a table near the window. The Brunswick Street strollers, who were mainly students, couples, and families, would peruse the displayed menu, and then continue their walk in the sunlight.

'Cappuccino thanks.'

Lola looked at the doorway. Ten minutes had passed. No sign of him. Was he late? Or was last night all about the marijuana coating the air? He sounded enthusiastic on the phone. She sipped on the cappuccino, enjoying the chocolate and the froth. The caffeine momentarily lifting her spirit, but only just. She held the cup close by her face.

Finally, a long-legged Aboriginal walked in. It was Kua. The strong-heeled stride hit the lacquered wooden floor with pride. He had just missed Lola.

A quick look around. 'Hi.' A smile beamed as he noticed her.

'Hello. I didn't think you'd make it.'

'Well, I'm here. Sorry I'm late, I was rehearsing with the band. But I'm not that late, am I?'

'No. How long have you been with a band? What's its name?' Lola caught herself asking too many questions before he even sat down.

'Six months. To answer your other question, Dark Spaces.'

'Interesting name.' She drank all the coffee. She placed the cup down and looked inside it. Suddenly, she felt naked without her social lubricant.

'What's with your drink?'

'It's finished.'

'You don't like things to finish?'

'No.' Lola wondered if he was asking a philosophical question. Perhaps he spoke in metaphors? Intelligent men apparently did that, not so much boys. Tony and Sam only knew how to be literal.

He went on more about the drink. 'If you drink slowly, you'll enjoy your drink more.'

Yes, and do everything else slowly. The cappuccino could definitely be a metaphor for other things.

'Maybe I drank too quick?' Lola felt she had done something wrong and appeared really uncool.

He smiled, relaxed, sat back. His body open. He put his hands around his neck. His slight up-tightness about being late soon relaxed into shattering charisma. He was even more attractive than he appeared the night before. His mood a bit different.

The waitress arrived at the scene of the two. 'Ready to order?'

'Sure.' He took his time at browsing the menu. 'Pineapple Tequila.'

He looked intently at Lola. 'So, let's talk.' Kua sat forward, face on arms resting on the table.

Lola went hot in the face. 'I live with my grandparents.' Bum, that's too honest …

'OK, you live with your grandparents.' He waited for more. The drink arrived. 'Thanks.' He sat up and sipped.

'Um, yes.' Her mind was ablaze with fascination, and she lost her trail of thought.

'And those girls?' Kua put the drink down.

What about me? She thought. She would go on to answer the question, nonetheless. She folded her hands together. 'They've always been there. I've been friends with them for a long time, since primary school.' She paused for a moment. 'How would you describe my friends?' She felt impressed with the adult-like conversation she was having with him.

'Well. They're responding to a force that they can't seem to be able to control. They can be immature. I think they're very selfish because of the state they're in.'

Yep, definitely smart, she thought. 'So how old are you?'

'Twenty-one.'

'And you?'

'Seventeen.'

'I'm not sure whether they lack substance or not. Paris is a real go-girl. Jasmin just follows her around like a puppy dog.' He looked out into the cafe.

'Why did you go with my friends that night?' The one-hundred-dollar question.

'I wanted to have them on. I played a game. They wanted me to be a mysterious Aboriginal. So I was, but then I left them dry.'

'Do you enjoy playing games on other people?'

'Only when they need to be played.'

'I see.' Lola stopped. She felt she had asked too many questions, but she felt unusually open and assertive, and needed to be.

'I tend to like older women, anyway.' Kua looked away and looked back, tapping the table briefly.

'Oh, really, older?' He was beginning to sound a bit complicated.

'Well, older women are at a certain level,' he gestured.

What level would that be? More experienced? Lola felt like she was starting to drown. She would have liked to ask him more about older women, but feared she would've sounded too insecure if she did. 'And what level are you at?' she asked.

'I'm interested in writing my music, playing my music, getting to know this land and helping my people. But I feel I've got to get to know all types. When I met you I thought that you're so outside the mentality of your friends, it was crazy.'

Lola smiled. 'I ran after you.' For a moment she felt she sounded dumb saying that. She hoped she didn't sound desperate.

'I was waiting for you to get out of that room. I had to walk so fast to get away from that bullshit house and your friends' smoke and mirrors life, I just couldn't stop myself. And it was just a matter of time when you'd come and chase after me. I was relieved to see you.'

So he really does like me? Lola sat back.

*

They emerged out of Blue Cafe with a balmy breeze hiding autumn. Brunswick street twinkling with shops and restaurants. The sky's pastel blue throwing a soft light along the street, with cars flashing past, and strollers staying with the same calm pace.

'Would you like to meet some friends of mine?' He cleared his throat.

'Now?'

'Yes.' He sounded adamant.

'Where do they live?'

'Well, actually, I've got a group of good friends here in Brunswick Street. There's a community hall of artists …,' he paused, 'they're creating an outback landscape, it's installation art. I've been working with them, doing sound tracks.' He stretched his arms.

So they walked up a few block ups. Lola was the only white woman with an Aboriginal man walking in Brunswick Street. 'This is it.' Kua pointed.

There was a cobble stone building and inside a group of Aboriginal people were working away at an Australian landscape so many squares along the expanse of a warehouse. Lola walked further in with Kua. There was the hushed sound of water pouring, and a meditative combination of other sound works emerging from speakers. 'I did the audio effects.' Kua nudged Lola's arm. The sounds and the display of desert-bush creating a strong sense of place. The snake painted along the walls shimmering and psychedelic.

Aboriginal sounds like didgeridoos, eucalyptus gum sounds, whipping bush sounds, fire, leaves, kangaroos hopping, kookaburras, and the works were there. Ubiquitous representations of Aboriginality. Lola noticed fat witchery grubs curling on a papaya leaf. Kua stayed beside her acting as a spokesperson.

'Are people going to eat them?' Lola asked.

'Of course.'

'How real is this environment?'

'It's pretty damn real.'

'Are the artists actually going to live here?'

'Yep.'

Women and men were standing near the rock representation of Uluru. A light above it would shine a colour spectrum symbolizing the varied colours of different times of the day that would normally be reflected on the actual rock. She also noticed that there were men in on one side of the rock, and women on the other.

'What are the women and men doing?'

'Traditional things.' It was a brief response.

'Right.'

When Kua wasn't looking, Lola sneaked from his side and stepped towards the women close to the Uluru rock, and watched them, partially covered by the indoor plants. They were older women. The women seemed sensitive to onlookers … they showed Lola that they were aware of her presence by glancing over, but not smiling. Then their attention would go back to what was holding their interest: the caves and water holes in the areas of the rock. The caves looked like birthing areas. The sign in front said "Women's Sacred Ground" with a picture of a camera with a cross over it. Apparently, a sign like this is to be found at the Uluru rock in Central Australia. Lola picked up a pamphlet.

Up until around 1996, anyone, including a white male, could walk up to the sacred female sites of Uluru and take photos, whilst at the same time no one could enter the male sites of Uluru, as there had been warning signs to stop the public from entering. The Government officials did not protect the female sites with signs and fences because a female government official was never sent to speak to the women who were the custodians of the female sites. Climbing the rock has generally never been approved by the Aboriginal custodians, but tourists still climb the rock desecrating sacred grounds. The problem is that the tourist industry allows it.

Nothing was actually explained about the significance of the sites for the Aboriginal people at Uluru, although most of it was new information for Lola. She didn't really know much about Aboriginal people, but intuitively sensed their cultural depth.

Kua would just look at Lola and wink. His wink hid knowledge. The Aboriginal Installation was a public space that covered a very private one. Self-disclosure was parlayed into nuances of 'I can tell you, but I can't fully tell you'.

Kua placed his arm on Lola's shoulder. 'Would you like to be an assistant in the studio? I'm going to do more sound effects.'

Lola always dreamed about doing something in the arts, whether it be writing or music.

'I'd love to!'

'In two weeks' time I'm going to go to my family. You're welcome to come. You'd get a real feel of the outback. You'd be living in a colonial settlement home. We're right in Alice Springs.'

'Oh wow. Yes. Yes, that would be nice.' Lola had never seen anything outside of Victoria. Lola looked at his young, ancient face, and felt immersed. It was just what she needed to hear. By going she felt she could get closer to Kua and his culture. Perhaps you had to show commitment to learning about a culture before being allowed into it. Was Kua testing her?

at home

Lola lived in a sanctuary of order tended to by her seventy-year-old Nonna, Elena. A woman obsessed with cleanliness and virtue, the floors were polished every day, dishes were washed twice after every meal, and clothes were washed twice in a washing round. Her Nonna followed her inner-promptings to live her life a certain way, and her values were consistent and unchangeable. And she loved everything that reminded her of Italy. She didn't like Berlusconi, but nonetheless, she had a picture of him hanging from the wall like she had pictures of all the Popes. The lounge room smelt of incense, was cool and well shaded, while the floors shone back light from the opening of the side of the curtain. A devout Catholic, she feared life without her religion. She loved her Nipote so much it hurt, the only daughter of her dead daughter, and her only grandchild. Her husband, Luigi, pretty much acted like an old time priest. He was a quiet man, who would get grumpy over food if it wasn't on the table by the time he was hungry. If he found himself hungry and outside of home, he'd eat anything in front of him, anything from curry, Chinese take away, Japanese, as long as the fish was cooked, and even Hungry Jacks. Elena only ate her home cooked meals. She had her own friends, but preferred her own cooking. The reality was that lack of hygiene just terrified her.

Certainly, Lola did not want to hurt her Nonna's feelings, nor did she want to worry her too much. But she knew that what she was about to undertake could shatter the life out of her little Nonna. She continued to pack as invisibly as she could in a house that was as pristine and quiet as a church. The polished wooden floor was best walked with socks, even slippers were too noisy. How would she approach her Nonna? She had run ins with her before. She thought of lies. She could tell her she was staying at Paris' place. Nonna thought that Paris was an innocent girl and whenever Lolina was out she must have been at Paris' doing homework or watching DVDs. God, if only she knew what Paris got up to.

But it would be too unethical to tell such a lie in this case, what to a woman who thought about becoming a nun when she was young. The door firmly locked, her ear on the door, she could hear her heart beating one thousand miles per hour as she listened to her Nonna coming from the lounge room. It seemed like she was walking towards her bedroom, which was right next to Lola's. One dangle of the rosemary beads and that was it. Lola was saying Omigod, Omigod, Omigod in her head.

The rosemary beads hit the draw. Quiet. Then a shuffling movement. It seemed like Nonna was now just standing there between the two bedrooms. She could have been trying to make a decision about what chore to do next, or had she noticed that something was different?

Suddenly a knock. Lola jolted from the door.

'Are you alright?' Nonna asked

'Yes.'

'What's wrong, you sound nervous.'

'Nothing.'

'What are you doing in there?'

She wasn't going to answer straight away.

'Packing up.' She bit the bullet.

'Where are you going?'

'Australia.'

'You are in Australia.'

'Another part of it.'

'Oh no! My Jesus! My Jesus! You're leaving.'

Lola sat on the bed trying to calm herself. 'Please don't worry. It's all going to be fine.'

'Let me in!' She knocked.

'I need to be by myself.'

'Please, let me in.' She knocked again.

Lola opened the door a little. Through the chink Lola could see Nonna's white hair. 'Talk to me!' Nonna grabbed the door.

'I'll, I'll be back soon.' She opened the door more, just to placate her. Nonna pulled it right open. Lola had never seen her so determined.

'As if. What happened to the Aborigine?' Nonna walked in scanning the room. 'Are you still friends with him?' Nonna now asked questions in a rapid tone.

'Yes, I'm still friends with him.'

'Are you going with him?' Nonna asked, probably already knowing the answer. Nonna put her hand to her heart like her heart hurt both physically and emotionally.

'Yes.'

'Oh, my Jesus, he's probably put a curse on you!' Nonna clasped her hands and looked at the ceiling. She was about to cry.

'No. No such thing. He would never do that,' Lola said trying to dissuade Nonna from a superstitious way of thinking she was prone to. She patted her shoulder. Nonna calmed down a little and sat on the bed next to Lola. Lola was now able to gather her thoughts better.

She spoke slowly and clearly. 'I'm going to go to the Northern Territory to meet Kua's family. When I get there I will phone you. I will be back, but I don't know when. I'll probably be back by the end of school holidays. I'm not a little girl, so please don't worry. Kua is a good guy.' There she said it, the way she rehearsed it in her head.

'But do you know these people? Where they live? How they live?'

'Please, Nonna, don't say anymore.' Nonna looked at her foot and pointed her toe up under her slipper as if to say, I don't know what to say. 'When are you going?'

'I've got one more day at school. Then I'm going.' Her Nonna just looked at her. A Mona Lisa smile appeared on Nonna's face. She lolled her head to the side, like a child, and gazed up at Lola.

Lola realized that it was getting close to the time where she had to make her own Nonna trust her as a responsible person, and this was the opportunity to do so. Lola had to grow up.

paris

Paris crossed her legs in the front row to the tune of the history lesson about world-wide slavery. The teacher, about forty-something, scanned the room at times, and at times seemed to be scanning Paris. But only just. But Paris obviously felt that she had captured the teacher's attention, and at times she seemed oblivious to what he was actually saying. Her intellectual, VCE look, with trendy glasses accompanied by a tweedish uniform, and albeit, blonde hair, appeared to temper Paris' inherent 'bimboism'. If she would go to university she would have to reconcile herself to a feminist-aware environment.

Would the teacher be attracted to her, as she poured out her viscous, sexuality? Or would he see through her? Lola witnessed Paris at work. Her legs crossing a few too many times … dress riding up. Being the patient friend she was, of course Lola would have to sit right next to her and put up with her narcissism. Paris wanted to get into politics and get into the media appearing like some sharp mind who would occasionally appear in Playboy magazine, but only because it was demanded, or by default because of a journalist's perv into Facebook, and his discovery of an image of Paris, which she, herself, would have uploaded if the guys who knew her hadn't already.

The truth of the matter was, Paris was a fake. The real Paris was drowning somewhere sixty feet deep. The only way she could be liked was by being a fake. She breezed through life by being compulsive. And she would breeze through her education through cunning. She would be looking forward to doing so many things at university, so many people to meet. It was for Paris' taking. Lola watched and watched Paris. She thought she had nothing in common for a long time. But Paris didn't pull her punches. She could get what she wanted. She was a success in her community of toughness and edgy sluttiness. She knew Landmark Education. Lola and Paris had been observing Landmark Education through Paris' twenty-three-year-old sister, Matisse. According to Landmark, you're supposed to follow what's right and true for you, and it doesn't matter what other people think. The idea is to be real. What was real for Paris was being an image of being a certain way. Paris was also competitively attractive. Lola would never admit to it herself, but she envied Paris and felt that she had something to learn from her, despite the fact that she recently had become an absolute egotistical bitch. But she knew that her days with Paris were numbered. Lola was not comfortable at being a fashionista tart, doing drugs for the sake of it, and sleeping with boys, for the sake of it. She knew she looked like a dork. Her inability to fit in was annoying Paris.

After the lesson on enslaved people Paris and Lola went outside to the cafeteria.

'You look better today,' Paris said whipping up a compact mirror out of her executive case and bringing it to her pink pout. Paris looked pretty enslaved to her own image.

'What do you mean I look better?'

'You don't look as tired as last time I saw you. Anyway, nothing make-up won't fix. Rouge will turn your paleness into cherry blossom,' she pronounced sarcastically.

'I don't think I look too pale.'

'You've got dark brown hair and really pale skin. Are you blind?'

Lola couldn't help but be more straightforward than usual. Matisse, while shampooing her long hair, had discussed the importance of being true to one's beliefs. Matisse believed that good skin and hair mattered just as much as one's political beliefs. Lola thought that Matisse followed Landmark Education for the wrong reasons, just like Paris did. Lola felt that being true to yourself meant being more honest. Her desire to be herself was now overriding her need for her friends. And as this desire was taking hold, she realized she didn't really need her friends, anymore.

So here was Lola's first attempt at being straightforward: 'Yeah, well maybe I am a bit pale but I'm not going to one of those tanning salons to get cancer.'

Paris looked away, as if she just noticed an insect coming her way and changed the topic. 'Can't wait to get out of this school so I can smoke whenever I feel like it.'

Silence.

'What happened with that Aboriginal dude?' Paris aimed her chin at Lola.

'Not much.'

Silence.

'Did you get into him.' Chin still up.

'Not yet.' Lola didn't want to sound like a prude.

'Don't you ever do it?' Paris watched for an answer.

'I will.'

'When?'

'When it feels right?'

Paris brought her eyes up. 'What bullshit is that! Perhaps you're one of those!' …

A strong piece of Lola's mind was about to punch through and cut Paris off her usual third degree about Lola's virginity: 'I CAN'T BE SUPERFICIAL IN RELATIONSHIPS THE WAY YOU CAN. I'M SICK OF YOU PESTERING ME!'

Paris stared at Lola. Almost one minute. Then it came: 'F--- OFF QUICK.'

Lola stood and bent towards Paris, 'I want to F--- OFF ANYWAY.' She walked away.

somewhere else

Wine-coloured earth looked like Mars in the morning from the corner of an awakening eye. Lola closed her eye, and then sneaked another look from her blanket. She realized Kua was driving on a dirt road in complete desert … somewhere away from the Stuart Highway. She spread her fingers through her hair, and ingested the red more. Dust rose as the car's wheels pressed against the ground. The mixture of dust and bareness cut a vista of how the end of the world could seem.

'You can get away from all that crap from Melbourne.' Kua turned his gaze away from the dirt road.

'Yes you're too right,' she stretched her arms. An inner glow started to beam inside her.

He stopped the Jeep. 'Let's feel the land.'

Lola got out, the sand crackled under her. She looked around. There was the panorama: purple-red sands, green, and yellow shrubs, the land appeared iridescent in colour, like the world underneath a dried up sea. She moved her attention back to Kua. He had bent down to pick up soil. He showed her the soil, his palm appearing soft and urban. Suddenly, the air felt like a tight brace on her face. The sky was bloody with thin clouds spreading along the horizon.

'Where do we go from here?' She squinted as the wind grew and started to blow sand.

'My place.' He flicked the dirt from his hands.

Kua parked the Jeep by a house, a dusty, gray house. The wind turned into a howling whistle going through the holes. There were older men sitting outside in the porch. 'These are my people from my tribe, Anangu,' Kua said. It appeared like they were watching nothing, but they were actually watching the land.

'Hello,' a man motioned to Kua and Lola. His skin was parched and leathery. 'Where are you from?' the man asked Lola.

'Melbourne.'

'Oh, bushfire place.'

Lola as a representative of a white person felt stupid and responsible for the fire problem in Victoria. Only Aboriginal people knew how to handle fire. If only everyone remembered that. The land would get very dry in Victoria, just like the land here. Lola looked out far into the emptiness. The sun's spider-like rays pierced her eyes as it got higher into the sky. Dust went into her nose and she smelt its memory of time. She spaced out for a second.

'Let's go in. You can meet my family and friends.' Kua placed his hand on her shoulder. 'Are you OK?'

'Yes. I'm just taking it all in.'

The house was large. A large area for eating with a long wooden table for quite a few people. Rooms right next to each other covered in pink Manchester and gray blankets. The nights seemed cold. A small television that might have been black and white. No phone anywhere. A lounge room made up of bamboo, its tropical nature seemed to be juxtaposed against everything else, the house in remote land, a hearth in the desert.

Kua's parents were handsome tall people in their fifties. Kua's mother's arms quickly wrapped around Lola's shoulders. Her embrace was sincere and welcoming. 'Somtink for hunger.' Kua's mum gestured to the table. Bread and butter were in the offing.

'Well.' Lola wasn't sure how to respond, although she was hungry from being on the road, and for days having to stop at service stations.

'Vegemite. Jam? Sweet or salty? Eggs maybe? We OK on this day,' Kua's mother announced, her strong hand showing the fridge and pantry.

'Right, nothing too much.' Lola tried to explain herself.

'When are they coming with the truck for food, Mum?' asked Kua.

'Tomorrow. But we still have enough for her to take.'

'Oh look, if that's your food situation, I don't need to eat now.'

'Don't worry missy,' Kua's mama smiled.

Music was playing on the radio, it was raspy and Jamaican, slow and sensuous. A fan was suddenly turned on. There was a woman near it. Her two kids were with her. 'Hey I wanna do it!' The youngest one pressed the fan off, just as the mother had turned it on. He giggled. 'Turn it back on!' his mother ordered.

'Turn on!' He pressed the button checking his mother with a wide smile. 'Now turn off!' He wanted to press again.

'Leave it on, that's it!' His mother pulled him away. 'Take your brother away from the fan!' The slightly older girl held her brother's hand, and took him to a nearby room.

'More toys are coming tomorrow. The truck's coming tomorrow. The truck has everything,' the woman said to Kua's mother. The woman looked at Lola, and then scanned her up and down. 'Hello. I haven't spoken to ya yet. My name is Arora. I'm Kua's sister. How old would you be? You look young.'

'I'm seventeen years old.'

'Your name?'

'Lola.'

'I'm thirteen years older than you, and I know a lot about the comings and goings here. You're not the first Kua's brought here, though. They go pretty quickly … and some stay longer. They go and come like the truck.' Her children came back from the room with some old toys. She held her toddler and kissed him.

Kua eyed his sister a 'you're not going to do this to me' look. 'Boyfriends come and go like the truck for you Arora.' He looked down. He shot again, 'Who knows where those kids come from?'

'Put a dirty sock in it … get real about life Kua. Get real will ya. You know that's not the case. Mr Easy you are!' His sister then rambled something under her breath as she placed the child on the mat over the cement. She grabbed a nappy from her bag.

Kua pursed his lips. He diverted his gaze from everyone. His parents stood away.

Lola walked onto the porch. So who was Kua? What was she doing there? She searched the far distance of the land to find the answer.

'Are you OK?' Kua walked up.

'Yes, I just keep away from all that.' She stared into the land.

'I'm sorry. I didn't think my sister was going to be here. Look at me, please.'

She turned to him.

'Don't worry about my sister … Um …' He wanted to explain more but couldn't. 'Let's go for a walk.'

'To where, where?'

'To somewhere.' So they walked to somewhere …

'What do you want from me Kua?' The ground scrunched under them.

'I don't know. A friendship? You're a nice person … but?'

'But what? Tell me what?'

'Well. It's hard to explain, but …' Kua's face looked jumbled up and red. 'You've come so far. You've come all the way here to be with me and to get away from your friends.' He waited. 'I can't be trusted.' He bit down on his lip.

'You can't? What do you mean you can't? In relation to what?'

'Let's walk a little bit further.' He put his hands in his pocket. 'I'm not faithful, not a one woman man. That's the bottom line. And you're a nice girl. Can you just be friends with me?'

'Yes, but.' Lola had never been on such an awkward spot like this. She felt like the insides of her were going to ravage her. 'I really like you, you know.'

'I'm pretty f---k-d up and I don't want to f--- you up. Let's walk further away.' They took a few more steps. 'I don't think we should have a relationship, I turn like the air, one minute I want meaningfulness, whatever you want to call it. Then I'll go around. I'm not into self-restraint.'

'You're an idiot.' Suddenly, she couldn't control the anger that was starting to well up, as the situation was getting really clear.

'Yes, I am an idiot.' He wiped the sweat with his sleeve.

Lola couldn't help but notice her sexual attraction to him, his scent and sensuality as he stood near her. His low voice, breath and trepidation. His concern. Her mixed-up anger. She felt roused to the point where she just felt like she was going to kiss him and take him on. 'You were going to sleep with Paris and Jasmin, weren't you? I really hate them.'

'No, I wasn't. I was thinking about it … but they were playing me … When I saw you I changed my mind.'

His physicality and honesty drenched her. 'I'm really confused now.'

'I'll drive you to the town, and there you could catch a train back.'

'No, no. I'll stay here and rough it out with you. Rain or shine with you.' She looked at him with the determination to win him over.

'We better go and have breakfast. My father's going to Darwin today for fishing. I think I'll go with him. My mother will look after you here. I'll talk to you again when I come back in a day or so …'

The rest of the day moved laboriously for Lola. Kua's sister left with her kids. It was a blessing, although Lola wouldn't have minded to talk to her about Kua's past. The house was quiet. Kua's mother was very nice and considerate. 'My daughter make trouble for you and Kua,' she said as she poured tea.

'No, it's OK. Lola looked to the side and said to herself under her breath, 'she told me what I needed to know.' Lola waited for nighttime. She wanted the first day at the house to be over and done with. Kua's return from his short journey was all that mattered.

Lola switched off the lamp and switched on the stars. It was a wash of stars surrounding her as she lay near the open window. Tears came down. The wind calmed, the moon skidding past scant clouds, and crickets burping under the frosty light foretelling some kind of a story. She felt angry, obsessed … and scared. She just stared out at the beauty, and followed a shooting star. When the star disappeared, she remembered her parents' trip back to Italy. The sky turned black.

Paris and Jasmin were always rebelling against their parents. They just didn't realize what it was like not to have them. Lola was only seven when they died. She needed them, to be safe in their arms. Kua's unpredictability brought her closer to the need for their arms. She hardly ever vocalized this need to anyone. It was good to know what she didn't ordinarily do. With this knowledge, she felt more attuned to herself. Everything after the plane crash was dark and void … and existing meant struggling from day to day until the struggle was forgotten in the middle of other people's lives … She was a voyeur. She watched other people live. And she had no one. She felt distant from her grandparents, at first they were too strict, and now they were too old, and too far away in their thinking, even though she cared about them. With this new understanding of herself, she closed her eyes.

the invasion

Lola opened her eyes. The window was gaping at her with a dragon sun extending its fingers behind clouds. She sat up, and wiped away the effect. Sheets of scaly red shot into view. A car from a distance could be heard, its growl growing bigger as it got closer, and closer. Lola rushed to the window. There was the car, it was speeding like it was on amphetamines, trying to break out of the razor blade sharp vice of sunlight. It spun out of control.

The car stiffened closer. It was a Datsun, a blue puny Datsun, Funnily it might have been Sam's car. It should not have been. But it looked like it was. Lola swallowed her saliva and felt its bitter taste. The reality hit her. The window was low enough for her to cut down. With vomity looking pyjamas on—she didn't care this time—she was off to face the friendship scam. The car looked like a wild animal trying to find its bearings.

Lola found herself turning with the car. As the car zoomed closer, Paris' glare surfaced behind her hair scrunching over her face in the wind. Jasmin was looking out in a Omigod laughing frenzy, her arms hanging out the window. Her hooker permed hair bouncing around her framework of over-done make-up.

There was Sam by the wheel with Tony near. Two boys with gelled back black hair, like a parody of each other pulling over the land, sun glassed like caricatures of the Blues Brothers. Some disjointed mouthing off from the boys before the car screeched to a halt. The four got out. Lola walked towards them. There was a coolness about them belied by the sway of alcohol. Jasmin's zing died a quick death as soon as she got out of the air conditioned beat up, her make-up melting to disgruntled clown. Paris' pearly French make-up quite out of season.

'What are yous doing here?' Lola asked.

Paris wiped her sweat from her forehead and briefly looked at it from the pulp of her palm. It was the first time Paris looked worked out, outside of her circuit of dance, sex and exercise. She squinted, the dust blowing around her stung her eyes.

'We're obviously in the right place, since you're here,' Paris announced.

'Where's the Abo guy?' Jasmin cupped her eyes and looked at the house behind Lola.

'How did you find out about here?'

'We got it from the Abo guy himself.' Jasmin's greedy lips smirked.

'Kua gave it to you?' asked Lola, incredulous at what was happening.

Paris nodded a yes. 'He hasn't given you the mighty puma yet, has he!' Paris stood akimbo.

'That's not funny.' Lola felt stripped of any value. And as the heat heaved around her, she smelt their lives and was reminded of the nightclubs, the thrashing of bodies that ventured out for freedom. A competition for expression. Endless sweat streaming down, and bottles thrown like dice on the floor, the stomp of some big guy slamming his way into your space. Dancing forever, and not getting anything out of it.

'You know where Kua lives?' Lola asked.

'Oh, that's his name!' Paris continued with her bitch stance.

'He gave his address to us the night we met him bozo. So what's your problem? You reckon he really likes you? He's into games.' Jasmin sounded clear and concise in her quasi-sober state. The smell of alcohol only a smidgen.

'He invited us too, wowser. So just relax. Let him dig you. We're going to let him dig us. Not the boys of course.' Paris looked behind her and did a snotty nose look.

'F--- off Paris. He could be my boyfriend you know!'

'Don't be so cupcake with him. Where's the dude anyway?' Paris lifted her neck to view.

'I don't know.'

'Can't we go inside the house? That's where your Kua lives.' Paris fluttered her lashes.

'No.'

'Don't be a bitch.' Jasmin pushed Lola. Her talons proliferating like those of a witch.

'I beg yours? Please don't do that. Don't push me, OK!' She held her hands up. Lola remembered the time Paris and Jasmin would nick her clothes during Sports period and throw them up a tree. It would take her ages to retrieve her uniform. She would walk around with her head up gazing at the treeline looking ever the desperado; then climbing the tree trying to earth the dangling shoes and dress, sometimes underwear on swim days. Once a dead beat, always a dead beat. Then there was the time she'd have to dodge blackboard erasers being thrown at her by other girls like they were hot turds off the dish. She'd end up wearing blue, pink and white on her hair and jumper. On the bus, as she tried to find a seat, she knew that she crashed into people's view as the 'dag', someone who stunk of being picked on. Girls whispering to each other on the bus only emphasizing her loneliness. If she defended herself, it would have been a case of an angry victim's fury. It was more cool to not react. She'd wait to go home to sob it off in her room. She was the girl who made Paris and Jasmin look so good. Go suck!

'Yeah, right.' Jasmin crossed her arms, and twisted her lip with attitude.

Lola waited as she thought of something important. Then she spoke. 'You need to be respectful towards his people. I think Kua's mum is in there right now. I'm not sure since I jumped out the window and didn't have a look inside the house this morning.'

'Relax wowser. By the way you look like shit in those p-jays,' said Jasmin.

'When are you going to get out of my life?'

'I'm sitting on trying not to hate you, at this moment. I'll tell you this, you can join the group again if you're not cupcake with the Abo guy.' Paris dropped her tongue.

'His name's Kua.' Lola didn't like 'the Abo guy' talk.

'Right Kua!' Tony said as he leaned against the car, arms folded, in cahoots.

'He walked away from our party because of you wowser.' Jasmin put her arm around Paris. Paris' blue catty eyes sized up Lola, as she was snugged under Jasmin's support. 'We can easily grab him away from you. You have no option but to be part of our group again. You haven't got what it takes for him to be attracted to you on your own,' said Paris.

'I don't wanna be friends with you anymore.' A fiery strength came over her that had originally pushed her to the outback. Lola suddenly Italianized with her hands, pointing her hand to her head, and then holding an imaginary loose screw. 'Do you get it!' She turned and locked the loose screw.

'We found him first. F--- off or be part of it!' Paris pronounced with her killer stare.

'What if I love him?'

'Oh, bullshit! Love? Are you f----d or what? You don't even know the guy! I wouldn't trust him as far as I can throw my cheatin Ol Man.' She kicked a pebble. Then continued. 'Guys are pricks. Even Sam and Tony are pricks.' Paris turned and winked. 'But we love 'em. They drive us everywhere. They're our friends, we don't f--- em, so it's different.'

'He's not a prick.'

'Right if he's not, asses don't smell,' Sam said by Tony's side, face like a placard, sniffing the surroundings.

Paris stepped closer. 'Where is he?' She breathed on Lola.

'I don't know.'

'Don't lie to me.' Paris looked behind her. 'Boys what shall we do with her?'

'Just piss her off. She's not worth it,' Tony announced.

'You go home!' Lola yelled back at Tony.

'Shut up and grow up!' Paris brought the angles of her cheekbones up against Lola's face.

There was the sound of a door quickly opening and shutting. 'What's going on here?' Kua's mother stood at the front of the house wearing a white dress with big purple flowers. Lola didn't speak. She walked up to the group. 'Who are these nutters?' She sized up Lola's face for an answer.

'They're Kua's and my friends ... sort of.' Lola looked away.

Kua's mum hovered over them in height. 'Hi just call me Snake. Kua's not here. OK. Now you rat bags can shoo.'

Lola realized that Kua's mum's English had changed and she wondered which way of speaking English was really her way, and if she had adopted two ways of speaking English to fool people, just like her son was into fooling people.

'We're not rat bags!' Paris exclaimed.

'Do you know when he's coming back?' Lola asked with a pleading look in her eyes she just couldn't manage for that moment.

'Yuk!' Paris checked Jasmin. 'Did you see that look? Give us a chewy.' She held her hand out and threw her eyes up. Jasmin passed the melted green wrap from her jean's pocket.

Kua's mother made her brow swagger. Both Paris and Jasmin were like identical twins wearing torn jeans and tops with pictures of a curvy Venus coming out of her shell with the head of Paris Hilton. She observed the boys dressed in gangland hip. She turned her lip up indicating she was a bit impressed. 'Hipster boys,' she said. She quickly spied the car. The car may have looked suss, like it could have been stolen.

'Nice beat up. I could do with a car like that?' Kua's mum laughed.

'Yeah, it's a cool car. It's been through a lot,' said Sam.

'Like a few accidents, toed away and sent back to the original owners, then stolen again from the original owners, then re-sold, and now, here's your little treasure.' She eyed it again. 'It's a trash convertible, but it's a sleek car. Hey, better watch it, I might steal it from you. So why don't you get back into this little petrol lover and zoom off?'

'We've been driving such a long time to see Kua.' Paris went into one of her stupendous moments. 'I mean all the way from Melbourne. But if you think we're in the way or anything, well, we'll go.' Paris wiped her face with a tissue from her Miss bag and made her chewing gum squeak with each large jaw movement. Kua's mum sniggered at the Paris monolith. Paris took a piece of paper out of her bag. 'Here's the note with his writing.' She blew a bubble. It quickly burst.

She read it. 'I've got a silly son. Well, come inside. And have some ice-tea. Give yourselves some rest before it's time for you to Buzz Off!'

The group followed Kua's mum. Sam smirked and Lola kicked him on the ankle.

'Just try to keep your gob shut. Our old uncles live with us,' Kua's mum said as she walked in front of them.

In the kitchen Lola's friends snooped around. 'Can't believe you live in the desert,' Jasmin announced to Kua's mum.

'They're Aboriginals dumbo,' Tony answered as he studied a picture of a coloured snake on the wall.

'I'm not a shit for brains!'

Sam turned his face to the woman's back as she poured ice tea by the bench. 'Hey, we don't need tea. We've got cold beers in the e-sky.' Sam grinned looking this way and that at his friends, winking behind the woman.

'No, it's all right. We'll have ice-tea.' Lola pronounced hands folded in front of her, a bit churchie. She sat at the table by herself while the others continued to amble around the kitchen.

'What are you kids really up to?' Kua's mum peered from the side of her shoulder.

'Nuffin much,' answered Sam. He suddenly whipped out a chair.

The others did the same with noise and giggles. 'Whose is this?' Paris threw an item she found from under her feet. A black Coles planet re-usable bag flew over the table. Lola's thoughts raced. 'I forgot to phone my grandma.' She went through the bag. 'I can't find my mobile!'

'Here's my mobile phone.' Paris took it out slowly from her Raphael bag and held it out with an up and down look.

'Thanks.' Lola pressed the numbers and then headed to the bathroom. The mobile shook and the voice eked through. She listened. 'Hi, it's me.' She raised her voice because Nonna was a bit deaf. 'I'm OK. It's hot here. What? I can't answer. Sorry I can't answer. These people are nice … I'll … yes, yep. I'll be back soon. Mmm. How's Nonno?'

'How's non non,' Sam could be heard saying.

'How's nong nong?' Tony answered back.

'Is that Asian?' asked Jasmin.

'Nong Nong means stupid,' Paris reported.

'Ha, ha! What does nig nog mean?' Jasmin laughed.

'That sounds f------ racist!' Sam hiccupped a fake laugh.

Wedged between them and the conversation, Lola tried to remain focused. She put her finger in her ear. 'Yeah. Yep. He's not here. He's gone away for a while. Don't worry … No don't.' Lola pinched her bottom lip. 'I'll let you go now. OK. Phone you soon. Luv you. Yep my friends are here. Yeah they're loud. Bye. OK. Ciao.' She looked at the phone and held the image of her grandma in her mind, and walked back to Paris to give her smart poo phone back.

Lola looked back at her friends feeling like a baccala. 'Have you phoned your folks?'

'Yeah, in the car,' Jasmin answered with her head on her arms on the table. 'I'm bored.'

A sweet tinkle. The ice-tea came on a fifties retro silver tray. Ta's and thanks came from the table. 'Nice children,' Snake lowered her head. They gulped the tea down in acid thirst that's meant for a beer. Sam burped, then Tony burped louder. They laughed. Lola watched them and watched for Kua's mum's reactions. Suddenly, a car screeched to a halt. Keys shaking. The door roughly opened.

Kua's mum put her cup down and walked to the entrance away from the kitchen. 'Who's car is that?' Arora's voice could be heard asking. 'Kua's friends,' Kua's mum replied. Then: 'Ringa, ringa—abrua, abrr, ringi. It sounded like Aboriginal talk no one really understood. It became high pitched and it sounded like the mother and daughter were arguing. Then Arora walked in from the lobby, frizzy hair high in a bun, strong jaw jutting out, a pronounced bust hovering over jeans. Nostrils widening. 'What are you people doing here?'

'Arora, these are mine and Kua's friends. We are waiting to see him,' Lola answered.

The Besties were stiff and smirking, like a school principal had walked in.

'OK, listen, I don't want no trouble from you lot.' She walked around the table. 'Trouble and I'll throw you out of here, put you in the middle of nowhere with the help of a few blokes I know around this area. Remember, you got no survival skills. You gotta behave in my parents' home or you're out.' Arora was a desert and urban woman. And she didn't suffer idiots. She could spot a liar a mile away. Kua had told Lola how Arora was a single mother, very protective not only of her children but also of her Aboriginal clan. She was tough, educated herself, kept away from grog. She tried to be true to her Aboriginal roots. The desert was in her soul. Its bareness flourished to life within her.

'No, no. We're fine. We're cool. No trouble, we promise.' Tony put on his reformed boy side. He had that thick coating of sounding considered and intelligent, when it suited the situation.

Sam's eyes were sliding off. All he was interested in was flouting rules and sounding moronic. A 'Whatever …' and 'Ha? 'And 'Like shit', 'Ass right real!' would have come from him to underscore any situation that required a more formal approach. He liked reading Freud for Beginners because he matched the description of id. He loved Kurt Cobain, but if Kurt Cobain were still alive he would have despised his reasons for liking him.

'Where did you meet Kua?' Arora asked Sam.

'You asking me?' He answered in a raspy voice, his eyes hidden behind the fringe he used as a curtain to hide his uncertainty when his hair wasn't slicked back in defiance.

'Yeah, yo wo, you!' She put on her Eminem rap voice.

Sam looked unimpressed. 'What was the question?'

'How do you know my brother Kua?'

'Ha. Umm. I met him through Paz and Jaz.' He motioned his head to point out the two girls sitting next to each other.

'And how did this Paz and Jaz meet him?'

'In Melbourne I think.' Sam's eyes were small and brown like puppy dog eyes, when they peeked through the dark fringe. Lola once had a crush on Sam. There was something sweet about Sam. A few years ago he was a cute sort of boy before his mouth developed into a dirt ditch. 'I met him through you right?' He looked at Paris. He wasn't going to mention the threesome that could have happened. He smirked.

'That's right. We met your brother in Brunswick Street. He's a very good musician. Dark Spaces is an awesome band.' Paris blathered on.

'Is that so. Is that what you truly think?'

'Yes.' Paris now sat upright like a preppy English school girl. Paris was supposedly self-realized through Landmark Education, but she was dumb in not censoring her arrogance.

The inquisition continued.

'What about you?' Arora took a step towards Jasmin. 'Love your hair, crazy hair right?' She touched it.

Jasmin moved away.

'Do you know what Dark Spaces means?'

Jasmin raised her eyes as she thought. 'Something to do with emos?'

'No, not really. Dark Spaces refers to the Aboriginal vision of the sky.' Arora looked up to an imaginary sky and caressed it with her palms. 'Aboriginal people don't look to the stars for inspiration, they watch for the dark spaces between them.' She glimpsed Jasmin and smiled. 'Betcha you never would have thought of that.'

'Nope.' Jasmin nodded and smiled back a little. Her hands coming together on the table. Jasmin was honest and transparent for a minute.

'My grandparents told me that. Have your grandparents ever told you anything?'

'Yeah … stuff like what people did in the fifties. Ha … What else?' Jasmin thought out loud. 'My mum told me how she does Botox on clients who are old and rich. And they walk around with paralysed faces afterward. There's heaps of 'em around. They're everywhere, and hidden. It's freaky. Who wants to be old?' Jasmin turned her gaze to her friends seated around the table and gave a crook, smug smile. Then her attention went back to Arora. 'She's a cosmetic nurse, my mum.'

'Interesting, what can I say?'

'Yeah.' Jasmin went stiff face.

The Besties chuckled.

Glances darted about. Minds opening up and then closing off again. Arora was more welcoming, after she said her night sky truth. She expressed a part of herself with a purpose. And she was standing there in a knowing space, while those who side-tracked life into a bucket of fun and grog sat in silence, wondering about the beauty of life. Smirks and giggles hiding shakiness. Finally, eyes closing off, feeling that childhood had now slipped away, and it was too late to go back.

Paris cleared her throat with a cough, 'So when do you think Kua will come back?'

'He'll come back some time tomorrow.'

'I see.' Paris sucked in her cheeks.

'Are you people going to have breakfast?' Arora clapped.

'We grabbed a bite at the service station.' Tony tapped his fingers on the table to disperse tension.

'I haven't had breakfast yet,' Lola said, 'I've been busy all morning with this lot.'

'What would you like, Lola?' Arora asked.

'I don't know. Vegemite on toast?'

'Yeah, we got that.' Arora coasted through the kitchen, and now appeared snug as a bug in her own home.

Soon after the meeting of minds, everyone was shown their room. Lola stayed by herself in the kitchen and ate calmly. Arora would have those Bestie Beasties under control for a while.

'This is like a special hotel,' Arora joked as she showed them rooms.

'Arora, put sticky on those mouths if you need to. Uncles need quiet and don't need to catch white nasties in their ears.' Snake sat down to rest her feet. 'Or I'll have to put them out to pasture myself—and they'll be carcasses in the morning.' She wiped her hands with a tea towel.

Lola in her room breathed in her moment again. From the window she could see the sunlight pouring over the desert in escalating beats. The early afternoon felt so shimmering and roasty. There was a breeze and there were sinuous clouds scattered along the blue. From inside someone had turned the radio on. It was a springy song sung by a young woman, 'loving you,' her voice flirted, then butterflies and flowers conjured up in Lola's mind with 'is easy cos your beautiful'. Lola pivoted around. She opened the cupboard door and spotted a long mirror. She locked the door and took her pjs off. She studied her bulbous boobs. Was one bigger than the other?

Lola had a lot of doubts about her body. She didn't have Paris' thin, sinuous catty figure or Jasmin's in-your-face curvaceousness. Her body felt unimpressive with its sloping shoulders and flattish bottom. Her eyes seeming perturbed at every window reflection, and her face pulled down towards the chin. She resembled her grandmother. In fact, she felt hunched over like an older woman because of her lack of confidence. She pretended to be neutral about the way boys didn't notice her, but it was a puncture in her night checking capsule every time they went out. She was named a dag; a hanger-on; deadbeat; and lezzo. She kept quiet in her room with CDS about feeling like shit. If she spoke to an older person about it, she would have worried that they thought she was suffering from depression. But perhaps feeling like shit was her style. She'd wear black like in mourning; she'd be a tomb of brain-screwed thoughts trying to make sense of Paris' and Jasmin's blinding light zapping through quick-fun-alley.

She grabbed her backpack and found her special dress. On, it presented a cleavage, and the dress was covered in small amber flowers, it was slightly A-line with laced arms and slender around the waist, meeting the knees with lace. She took out newly bought kohl from her newly bought Chinese make-up bag and proceeded. She aligned her eyes to the mirror and began to experiment. She elongated her eyes and made them look tigress, with the green from her hazel becoming accentuated. Her eyes openly smouldering. Then she took out small scissors from her make-up bag, and cut away at the long fringe. She styled it into a short crisp even cut that framed her eyes and made her face look more round and perky. The effect was great. The rest of her hair long and straight. She took an orange band and put it around her forehead. She put on some light plum lip gloss.

A desert princess smiled back at her. Somewhere between Hippie and Indigenous, but not necessarily Aboriginal, just more freedom-loving and different.

This would be her stance: Try a different approach, be more relaxed. This attitude would accommodate and safely attract a relationship—it could grow organically, it would not have to be pushed. She had been doing it all wrong. Perhaps she could be somewhere between what she was in Melbourne and the way her friends had been without having to have that Kings Cross neon grab.

Suddenly, 'Besame Mucho' was winding into the airwaves, languishing and Spanish riding through the window. Her grandparents would listen to this one—one of their old favourites. Lola noticed the desert took on the colours, moods, music, people that surrounded it. It was Aboriginal mixed with everything else, including the multicultural desert girl she felt like. Outside the window, an old man sat with the radio beside him. He sat under the shade in the a porch. He was studying the land. He seemed to be studying 'Memory'. Aboriginal people have been heavily influenced by Dreamtime.

Kua spoke about Dreamtime. Aboriginal people respect it greatly because it tells the story of the land and the ancestors who lived on the land. The ancestors are spirits that weave stories and images together and try to speak to those living. It's Aboriginal collective consciousness, and it's timeless. Aboriginals can read the land in a way that non-Aboriginals can't. Firstly, they see the land as sacred, and believe that no one in particular owns it. White people, on the contrary, believe that land should be bought. This has been a contentious point in Aboriginal Land Rights.

The old man sitting by the porch took out two sticks from his pocket and began to hit them together. A song travelled from him. The song inflecting the continuous beat he was producing with the two sticks. The beat could be felt echoing through the ground. As in the case of synaesthesia, which means blending of senses, what you hear and what you see become one, it seemed like the sound etched its way into the gum trees and gave the desert a language. Lola watched him from her hidden position by the window, wishing that she could make contact with him. She felt grounded by the beat. She felt renewed.

Lola stayed by the window watching the unfurling of the day. She would rather do that than deal with her friends' peccadilloes.

Kua came back with his father at night carrying bucket loads of fish from Darwin. Paris and Jasmin, Tony and Sam were frisky on the porch pushing for distractions. When Kua saw them he looked very surprised.

'What are you all doing here?' Kua's turquoise piercing on his ear shone under the matted light of the porch. Insects buzzed around the light with a continuous hiss cutting the air. Kua's father scanned the scene and gave an annoyed grimace to his son, and then he carried the fish inside the house. Kua avoided his look. His attention went back to the visitors.

'Sorry I smell of fish.' Kua took a hanky out of his pocket and wiped sweat dripping from his face.

'We came to see you, what do you think by the way?' Jasmin flapped her arms out and crossed her leg over the other one. Now she was wearing a jarringly tight-fitted red vinyl dress. She looked like carnival on legs.

'Did I invite you?' Kua furrowed his brow in jest, as he patted his face.

'Yes, you did.' Paris walked up to him injecting a smile. She was wearing a lacy white dress with a eucalyptus leaf stuck with sticky on the left boob.

'Where did you get that leaf?'

'I walked to the trees during the day. In the heat by all means.' Paris pouted and caressed her leaf. She did look an ounce silly, but she didn't care.

'Oh, must have been hard.' Kua teased. Then he glanced over Tony and Sam. 'How are you?' He wiped his hand and then offered his hand to one, and then to the other one.

Tony turned it into a 'give-me-five' on Kua's hand, and rattled on with facts. 'We got the grog here mate. This place looks shit boring. Agree dude?'

'No.'

'Do you have any girls around here we can chat up?' Tony slapped Kua on his shoulder. 'Sorry to be so straightforward, mate, but we've come a long way and we've been waiting a long time. If there's nothing to do here, you better tell us now.'

'It's so fucking boring here.' Sam just confirmed Tony's attitude. Sam took a smoke out of his pocket and lit it up. His hair was now slicked back just like Tony's.

'It's not boring, it gets pretty packed here. The girls here live in the bush. So you gotta go and look for them,' Kua winked.

'Where are these chicks? Who can see them?' Sam shook his hand and took a step down from the porch and walked towards his car.

'Hey, listen, come back, it's just a joke.'

Sam nodded as he walked to his Datsun. His Datsun was a trusted friend.

'Come back.' Kua took out a cig from his jeans and lit it. Paris walked up and grabbed it. 'Your cigarette feels hot.' She dragged in the smoke and slowly blew out in his face. As Lola watched from the window, she felt she could do with a few buckets.

'What are you doing?'

'I'm blowing smoke in your face,' Paris said with a put-on velvety voice.

'Is that supposed to mean something?'

'If you think so.' Her voice remained a veil floating in the air. What a bitch! Lola thought. If she was any greener with envy she would have turned into a creeper that would just keep growing from the window she was listening from. She would find herself grow around the house until she'd wrap herself around Paris and strangle her—to death.

Kua looked out to the boys. 'You don't have to go home, stay another day. I'll take you to places around here tomorrow, and we'll have a party later.'

What are you playing at? Lola wondered.

Tony nodded an inconspicuous 'yes' to Kua as he stood between the house and the car. He took a step back to the porch. Sam followed from his Datsun position like a dim sim expecting to be fried. 'Spin me round! What's over here that's entertaining?' Sam asked.

Kua took out another cigarette from his pocket. As he lit it, he said, 'Party, grog, party, grog. How many times do I have to say it?'

'Convince us.' Tony threw a glance.

'I will.' He pitched the unfinished cigarette into the sand to motion action. Then he suddenly felt distracted. He looked around the porch. 'Where's Lola, Paris?'

Lola's insides curled up as she heard him say her name. The voice was close to the window.

'Your cupcake is inside the house. She's feeling sorry for herself in her room. You better go and see to her,' Paris said in a sing-song voice.

'Get the condoms ready,' Jasmin laughed.

'As subtle as a sledge hammer.' Paris smiled at Jasmin.

Lola scurried from the window like a possum, and in the dark, hid in the bed. She didn't answer to Kua's rasp on the door. Her mind sank into a race against itself.

Kua went back to the porch. As Lola heard the voices rising, the situation was prevailing as one of indecision. Kua seemed caught up with trying to impress the Besties. Too curious to fall asleep, she sneaked back to her convenient window posting. It had gone quiet. Everybody was sitting on the porch waiting for something to happen. The moon was almost full and almost mad, and the crickets were the ones really hailing the night.

'Why don't you show them places, Kua?' Arora interjected casually from the doorway. The older people were chit chatting in the kitchen.

Kua's feet were shuffling. 'Sleep over. We'll go sightseeing and then we'll do a Corroboree.' He eyed the group from his wavy hair.

'What's that mate?' Tony leaned on the railing by the side of the porch.

'It's kinda like a party.' Kua answered. 'Of course then there's the real party.'

'Talkin about partying makes me tired. I'd rather do the real thing. I'm shutting off for tonight.' Tony walked back into the softly lit house. The others dragged their feet back inside.

Feeling a bit too bored and tired was defining the night. Lola rested under the blanket. The last thing she heard was Jasmin saying, 'Go rub.' Then some last minute laughter from the boys. Then it was all silent. The moon facing Lola for some reason smiling brilliantly. It didn't quite make sense.

Morning flooded in with a hoot and a twirl coming from the different rooms. Lola decided that she would walk down the corridor with a distinctly forlorn look on her face on the way to the bathroom and breakfast. Kua would notice her and she would ignore him. She wasn't one to play games, but this behaviour was called for. She needed ammunition against the hullabaloo of Paris and Jasmin. The bubble of fun they created would trap everything in its wake, leaving all dumbfounded and overwhelmed. She knew better. She remembered Paris' and Jasmin's polished little lezbo dance in nightclubs. It was an eye grabber killer floor show, it had everybody watching incredulously, boys salivating in wonder at what was going on, and girls feeling uncomfortable. They would gyrate and pash to get into the minds of others, to have an Effect. The whole thing an attention spin that splashed of 'we're up for anything boys, we are fun!' After a dance like that, all the boys ignored Lola. Lola would fidget, straddling along the sidelines, feeling like some creepo friend.

At the long table laughs, giggles and wisecracks grew in magnitude. Kua was participating in such an annoying way. With 'F--- ye', 'Shit ye', 'Going nowhere man.' He sounded like the immature Sam still looking for his mind behind his ass. Where was the staunch individuality he showed that night she met him? Was he playing a game or was he really taken in by the four's hoopla? When Kua left the breakfast table, it was time for the Besties to de-brief.

Jasmin took out a Girlfriend magazine from her large bag with a picture of an orangutan dressed in a pink tutu. She started scanning through pages. 'How come there are no pictures of Abo chicks in mags?'

'Cause there are no Abos in modeling,' answered Paris. 'They don't wear bras so their tits probably sag.'

Lola's face tangled up. 'Shut up before anyone hears you.'

'No f-----,' Paris whispered, 'they have certain standards in the Modeling Industry, you know. They can't accept everyone. Waist, tits, arse got to be in proportion. Got to have high cheekbones, too.'

'You view yourself as a model, don't you Paris?'

'Look, don't hate me for being confident—but I've got the right characteristics and features. I know I do. I can't help it. So many people tell me I should get into modeling. It's not funny.' Paris' voice sounded all husky, like she did rounds of smoking and hard work in the career of being herself and the research involved in it, like some New York journalist. A slick professional at being a chick. 'I reckon so many girls hate me for being good looking.' She paused, and flicked her hair. 'I'm just being honest.'

Lola continued with the topic. 'What about Jasmin?'

'Zoo mag,' Paris retorted.

Sam and Tony chuckled.

'No, I'm serious. Why are you laughing? That's what she's suited to. It's not funny.'

'It's modeling.' Jasmin studied the idea.

'What about me?'

'You're going to hate me for saying this.' Paris lifted her top lip revealing a stiff smile. 'Woman's Day'.

'What?'

Paris continued with her insight: 'Some kind of story about you and your grievances. I can imagine you in one of those magazines my mother would read.'

'That's not sexy.' Lola frowned.

'You'll be the youngest person amongst middle-aged gropers.'

'They're all going through menses,' Sam observed.

'Menopause you mean. My mother gets that. It's like you're on fire or somethin. Like your c--- is on fire and you can't cope.' Paris breathed in. 'She grows a mouth too, you know, with all these shitty comments about everyone and everything she knows. She goes on about how she's been used in life. That's my mum. She's right too. My dad's a prick.'

'Off the topic of your mum and dad. Why do you have these ideas about what's good looking and what isn't. Isn't it relative?'

'The truth is there.' Paris pointed her hand outwardly, like there's an imaginary fashion God that presides over all of us.

'Everyone's got different opinions, but.'

'Everybody knows what's good looking and what isn't, Lola!'

'What about Kua? Do you reckon he's good looking?' Lola sneaked the question in.

'Kua is hot model material. If it wasn't for his looks I wouldn't be here.'

'Is that the only reason why you're here?'

'Pretty much ... and to see what it's like in these out-backy places. But,' Paris lowered the corners of her mouth and looked around her, 'there's not much here, it's a shit hole.'

'The red's wicked.' Jasmin poured water from the jar onto a glass. 'Red's my favourite colour.'

Tony crossed his arms on the table, and leaned his head on them. 'Red. What is there here but red?'

'There's some green because of the rain,' answered Lola.

'So, big deal. You just walk further out and you can see it. What else is there?'

'A red arse,' Sam blurted, his face a blanket of general anaesthetism.

'What do you mean!' Lola demanded an answer.

'If you walk around like Abos in a g/string.'

The Besties laughed. As the laughter subsided, Lola cut in, 'I haven't seen anyone wearing g/strings.' She remembered to whisper. 'It's something you must have seen on TV.'

Kua came back into the kitchen, whipped out a chair, and straddled it. Discussion of the topic stopped.

'Where did you get your earring? It's really cool,' Jasmin asked.

'Some Brisbane fare,' Kua said. 'Is that your natural hair?'

'I got it done.'

'Where did you get it done?'

Paris snared the answer, 'She got her perm done at Westfield Shopping Centre.'

'Bullshit Paz. It was at Eastern Scotts in Brighton.'

'It looks like a Westfield Shopping Centre job.' Paris bent her fingers and studied her silver nails.

'What's wrong with it?'

'Not much.'

'Oh.'

Paris looked up from her nails. 'Don't worry hon. I like it. It's just that the perm locks look a bit too tight.' Paris held a bit of Jasmin's hair to emphasize her point. 'It's a bit too eighties.' She let go of the hair.

'And all this time I thought you loved it.' Jasmin looked distinctly upset, her mouthy gloat about to descend into a frown.

'Jaz. I'm sorry hon. I mean it's almost perfect. Almost perfect hair for a hair spray commercial …' She paused. 'You know, my father, being a politician and shit deals with actors, media and all that.' She paused again. 'He's been to parties and met people and … f----- around, too, by the way.' She twisted her lip quickly, then went back to studying her nails. 'And they look similar to you.' Her voice kicked high before going back into its smoky underbelly.

'Who does?' Jasmin pouted.

'What I just said. People in the entertainment industry are just as beautiful and kooky as you are. LOVE YOUR HAIR!' Paris' face froze into a smile.

'OK.' Jasmin sat back a bit relieved. Jasmin noticed Kua's hair and ran her fingers through it. 'Abos … I mean … you guys have wavy hair.'

'Yep.'

'And wear contrasting colours. Well, as you are right now.' Paris narrowed her eyes to study Kua's terracotta T-shirt and white jeans ensemble.

'No we walk around naked. Or we should more often.'

'Do tell.' Paris folded her hands together and plonked her face on them.

'What if I take yous for a tour around here. We go see Uluru?'

'Nu! Well maybe!' Tony munched on his Wheat Bicks, milk slashing out of his mouth.

'Common you'll love it.'

'It's just a rock.' Sam blinked fast.

'Let's go and see it. It's probably beautiful.' Paris enthused. 'I've seen pictures of it, it's awesome. But then again. Why does it have to be today? It's too hot.' Her niceness snapped into an executive decision.

'Yeah. So what are we going to do?' Jasmin glazed over an empty glass.

'Tonight Corroboree and party after-wards!' Kua flashed his pearly whites.

'Now that sounds good.' Paris agreed.

And her Besties did, too.

In the centre was a flame against the pitch black, the night air moving through the dance moves. Stomping white painted bodies searching for ancestors, moving, singing, jabbering, with the repetitive tapping of sticks. The didgeridoo wailing into the ground vibrating under you, grounding you, saying something to you. The dancers in a trance. Their moves inexplicable, continuous. Then bodies shifting around each other again with purpose. The dance then stopped.

Smiling and handshaking took over. The dancers were friendly and aware, appreciative of the audience. Paris and Jasmin watched without saying anything, Sam and Tony, too. They seemed almost impressed at something again, outside of Arora's explanation of the Dark Spaces.

The sand was cold. The desert cooled down at night. Lola watched, cardigan on. The whole evening felt sacred. Lola wondered if she and the Besties were intruding a little. Corroborees are presentations, but also exclusive events. For it was Alice Springs. Aboriginal Land. Where did Kua fit into this? Lola crossed her arms as the desert nipped at her. She was diving into a space perhaps of some special metaphor about cross-cultural relations? Perhaps a metaphor about human desire? Whatever it was—she looked up—it played out in the night-scape twinkling with stars, and knowledge buried within itself.

Kua shouldered up to Lola's friends. He ignored her as she ignored him to keep the facade of distance. But where did he belong? How could he bring people together when their very fabrics were so divergent? Paradoxes that skirt around each other, rather than meet and reconcile into some artwork of beautifully shaded differences.

Australia seemed like a hotchpotch of things. Kua was living proof of an attempt to be himself and everything else. The beauty was in his eyes as they may have insulted with their desire to be reflected back, to be defined. So he looked at everyone, 'Let's get some drinks!' He'd raise his eyebrows and smile. The grog was there. Tony and Sam ran to the boot and took the e-skies out. They started to grow back into their western personalities. 'It's 'bout time!' Sam let out a huge sigh. Paris and Jasmin were quick to sign on. It was going to be a party night in the desert. The allure of the night attracting all like animals emerging from their enclosures ready to live, and transgress over those who are sleeping. The beer cans crashed open into a flame that went down the gut dissolving all differences.

Tony flicked on the music. The car shimmered with the beat of trance. Kua jumped on a rock. His lithe body silhouetted by the moonlight as he began to ride the beat, entering its whips, its shakes, its crystal tings, moving his hands against whatever rained on him. His long legs looping around, his smiles secretively offered. His tongue sensuously displayed from time to time. The others joined in jumping up and down. A gallery of shapes forming by the drill of the moment. Sand pounded on. Lola shaking her head inside the swell: she was starting to feel at one with the others. Paris and Jasmin gyrating crazily by Kua's side competing for attention. Jasmin's large bust shaking whorishly in tight vinyl. Paris' in a bra-less state with nipples displayed behind her white transparent dress. Lola tossing her desert dress from side to side. The girls moving against each other. Paris and Jasmin holding each other's arms, rocket riding together, trying to stitch a centre for their lesbo act.

Lola spun her dress around—the dress brushed against the duo. Jasmin pushed Lola away. 'You dance shit. You don't move to and fro. It's the beat you got to follow.'

'Forget it.' Lola stopped dancing, then flapped her arms and walked off.

Lola sat by herself on a rock. Kua noticed what had just happened and came off the stage. Lola was impressed with his show of disappointment. Lola offered a quick glance. He returned the glance with a nod. At least he never got to witness the Paz, Jaz floor scramble.

Tony turned the volume down, the trance mood left to the background. 'Let's get more vibrators.' Tony opened the boot of the car again. He passed the cans around. They were crashed open in fury. The Besties took a full hit in thirst.

'Lola drink!' Jasmin gave a sarcastic grin and whisked the drink quickly over to her. Lola caught the slippery blue just before it would escape her and make her look slow. She held it up by the fire and opened it, and knifed Jasmine a look. She swigged it down a bit, and then a bit more. Its bitter sweetness opened up within her like a Chinese vegetable. It was the second time in her life she'd drunk alcohol. This time it tasted much better, the first time it was in a dingy nightclub. Perhaps it was the night air or the moment. Tonight was not going to be Paris' and Jasmin's night. She would kill them for tonight. Paris and Jasmin were, thank God, so far just playing cats in the sand.

She wanted to be a more 'open desert girl'. 'Open desert girl' had to stop being a wowser. But she wasn't going to grog herself up to oblivion. She would be neutral and enigmatic to others. If only the others allowed her to own a more attractive personality other than the 'dag'. The dress hadn't done much so far, except stop the Paz and Jaz dance. And the smoky eyes she wore all day—who knows what they were going to do?

Kua didn't cast his eyes in her direction again. And she would not react to him in case she would scare him off, and that would make him turn to the sexual libertines. But when Lola did manage to check him, he seemed calm and cool, even as he watched and drank and studied Paris' and Jasmin's antics. Whether he was sure of what to do or whether he had not made up his mind, was yet to be seen. Kua was hard to fathom. And Lola liked him even more because of that.

'Hey, have you ever met a girl who does fanny farts when she's pissed?' Paris wailed.

'No.' Kua drank and gave a big burp.

'Here's the girl.' Paris pointed to Jasmin.

Jasmin looked at Paris and laughed her beer out of her mouth. 'Don't remind me.'

Lola remained seated on the rock and thought about how crass and obvious Paris and Jasmin were. They were vultures. 'Hey Lol, don't be so cupcake about you know who,' Paris said out loud. 'Come here with us, princess.'

'No thank you. I'm happy here on the rock.'

'You look like you're trying to do a shit. You look constipated.' Jasmin looked up from the boot of the car as she took out more cans.

'I beg yours!'

'Get up and join in.' Paris walked up to her.

'But I'm happy sitting here.'

'What's wrong with you? Maybe you should go to bed, it's probably your bed time.'

Lola didn't answer back.

'I'd like to know why you hate us, and why you hung around with us for so long?' Paris secured her foot on the rock Lola was seated on.

'I don't hate you, I just decided to move on.'

Tony and Sam started clapping, straight away. 'Bitch Fight! Bitch Fight!'

'I don't want to be part of this.' Lola got up.

'You are part of this.' Paris quickly pushed Lola back. Lola almost tripped backwards against the rock.

'Look. Please don't. I never hated you. I don't hate you.'

'So what's your issue?' Jasmin walked up.

'I'd like you to stop stalking me.'

'We told you already we were invited here by Kua himself, and were not stalking you bitch!'

Tony and Sam found cue to continue with their chant: 'Bitch Fight! Bitch Fight!'

'I have a right to stop being friends with you without having to put up with all this shit.'

'Tell me one thing Lola, why did you hang out with us for so long?' Paris dug her long manicured nail into her forearm.

'Ouch. Don't do that please, don't do that.' Lola flicked her arm away.

'Paris stop!' Kua took a step forward.

Paris looked back. 'Keep away.' She turned her attention back to Lola. 'Tell me why did you hang out with us?'

'Because I thought I could learn something from you. I thought you girls were cool. You're so smart Paris.'

'Yeah, and …?' Paris stared.

'I thought you knew more about guys and sex and stuff. And you don't suffer fools. God, Paris what do you want me to say to you?'

'What else?'

'Jasmin's so free, so funny, with her fanny farts.'

'Well thank you slut.' Jasmin smiled.

'But what went wrong?' Paris looked around as if searching for the answer.

'Bitch Fight! Bitch Fight!'

'Shut up!' Paris brought her hand up.

'You're too full on. I need to be by myself. I don't know maybe one day we can be friends again …'

'It doesn't look like you can meet our standards.' Paris dug her silver painted toe nail into the sand.

'You know. I just can't take it anymore Paris. Your constant questioning whether I've had sex or not. I get that from my grandmother, but she wants me to be a virgin, you want me to be a slut to fit into your group.'

'I told you, my Ol' Man is an absolute cheat. I don't trust guys, I only trust whatever they have to offer for the moment. I enjoy my slut philosophy.'

'Onya Paz!' Tony gave a fist to the air.

'I know what you mean.'

'Do you?'

Lola felt really awkward saying this: 'Do you remember the Feminism class we had in English? How it looks like Feminism is dead and all that?'

'Yeah, I remember.' Paris did a hurry up, 'what are you going on about?' gesture with her hand, and took a quick sip with the other.

'Why do you?' She paused. 'I just wonder …'

'Get on with it!'

Lola looked up to the sky, 'Why do you act the way you do?'

'Like what?'

'Like,' Lola paused, 'you know dress the way you do and stuff. You're just catering to males. You see yourself as a commodity.'

Paris stared like she was hit by a meteorite. 'Big word psychologising wanker you are! Well, I'll be a big word psychologising wanker, too then. Yes, I am a commodity. I am my own commodity. I am of my own making. I'm in control of my own life. I'm not controlled by men.' Paris held herself up straight and crossed her arms.

'I think you're sort of not controlled by men. But on a wide, Feminist scale you are.'

'Feminism sucks. It's so boring. Who wants to be a dick-strap-on chick listening to boring love songs at pool tables?' Jasmin shot.

'Omigod. What have I started?' Lola pounced her forehead with the pulp of her palm. 'Not all Feminists are dykes. And anyway, so what if someone is. Look, if it wasn't for Feminism, there would be no rights for women. Feminists created the right to vote, and the right for equal pay and the right to have childcare, you know … and all that shit,' she shook her head. 'Like, you know …' her voice trailed off.

'Yeah, I know, but I'm a Feminist in my own 'man-made' way.'

'That's a silly paradox,' Lola declared. 'I hope paradox is an acceptable word for you.'

'Paris is a ho. Hos are dumb.' Jasmin laughed. She kicked the sand hard. She was compelled to disperse energy. The topic was heavy. She plonked herself on the ground and felt around for another can in the sand.

'I know what a paradox is,' Paris mouthed to herself. 'What about you? Do you reckon you're a Feminist?' Paris kicked a bit of sand at Lola.

'I don't know. Kind of.'

'You're a miss-goody-two-shoes. You'd make a nice little wife.'

'That's what my grandma wants.'

'What about you? Do you wanna be a servant wife?'

'Of course not, definitely not a servant.'

'Don't you wanna have fun?' She eyed Lola with a small smile, and held the can up and let the beer drip over her tongue.

'Yep, of course.'

'I think me and Jasmin are more Feminist than you?'

'Sort of. There are different types of Feminist, like different types of women.'

'Girls can you just shut the f--- up! This is boring!' Tony pleaded.

Paris gazed at Tony with a fierce look. 'No. Girls are not just going to shut the f--- up. We're talking OK!'

'Paris is a skanky ho. Aren't they supposed to be dumb? Ha?' Jasmin rubbed her face reminding herself of what she had said a moment ago. Empty beer cans were piling up in front of where she sat. 'Paris is not dumb though,' she said to herself softly. 'She's smmart …'

Paris held her latest can to her mouth. She swooped it down in a few seconds flat. 'Woow … Yeah, I'm proud to be a skanky ho. We get ahead. Sex rules. The rest is a bullshit cover-up, anyway.'

'What do you mean?' Lola narrowed her eyes.

'F--- rules.'

'On ya Paz!' Tony raised his beer.

'I'm lifted from the dirt with beer f---s, f---s and f---s. The rest is bullshit. It's all an image, an image of it not being there, but it's really there.' Paris searched for a full can along the sand.

'What do you mean, "not really there, but there"?' Lola asked again.

'So speaketh the thesbian,' Tony declared before his mouth welcomed more beer.

'God Lola, you're a sucky bore. Does everything have to be explained. You from that hardworking ethnic shit … You're so f-----, f--- what's the word?'

'The word's f--k-d,' chuckled Sam.

'Thank you.' Paris genuflected. Then she pointed at Lola. 'She's always,' Paris closed her eyes for a moment, 'as straight as a?' … Paris burped, 'as a normal person.' She laughed.

The thought then swept her. 'I don't want to be normal.'

'You're not normal!' Jasmin stared up from her pile.

'Be cool.' Sam took a break with a cigarette. 'Be cool Delores,' he said. 'Why don't you call yourself Delores?' He put one hand on Lola.

'I'm just trying to talk to someone, but no one is listening!' Lola hid her face in her palms.

What was it about everything? Nothing made sense. Whenever she'd try to speak, no one was there. It was too lame to have a thought. It was too cigless and grogless. It was uncool to have a discussion about anything. The only place Lola wanted to be without words was when she was one with the land. When the desert peaked in redness at midday. When a flash of something whipped in the distance behind eucalyptus leaves. When the faraway flight of birds showed the way to an oasis. And when termites whitespread dead wood. And fried animals in slumber rose to a pitch as they became carcasses with crawlies shimmering in the sunlight. When the night rush hushed into your ear and crickets rasped under your ground.

Aborigines knew their gut. They knew things by walking on the ground, by knowing where water hides, by being 'present'. They didn't really need grog like they thought they did. Kua's knew his way when he allowed himself to be Aboriginal. He looked confused when he was trying to be different. Sure, he seemed cool with his turquoise earring, and the twirl end of his hair rusty coloured. His kind of exotic beauty a Bento ad. He played on his worth. Everything in society is worth its image. If it wasn't a transferable kind of commodity, something that's fuckable, edible ice hot on the eye, good to be seen with, it wasn't worth anything. Paris was a Macbitch. Her dad was a politician, an economic rationalist, and she was a relationship rationalist, a man rationalist. Woman on top a sesame seed male—well-hung. Lola felt she had little worth. She never blasted into any scene, into any kind of acceptance. She knew that Aboriginal people were left in the lurch. That big society hadn't fully acknowledged them. So Kua was a muso, so Kua acted spiffy. She figured him out. He could be his Aboriginal self with her because she was an outsider, too.

'Go grind against a gum tree …' Sam pointed at the tree. 'It's ready and waiting.'

'Shut up will ya!'

'Here's something that loves you, a tree. You don't have to feel sorry for yourself anymore just because your parents are dead.' Paris stared.

'You're gonna get gang-banged one day,' Lola sprayed the words.

'What!' Jasmin smiled and looked around.

'Lola knows what that means?' Tony pulled open another can.

'It almost happened.' Paris took out a cigarette from her Raphael bag. She lit it and took a drag and slowly blew out remembering the experience.

'When? I didn't know about this.' Jasmin frowned.

'You were sick or something. It was like Grade Six. It was raining outside during lunch time. The boys ganged up on me under the teacher's desk and grabbed me and shit. I was worried that I was pregnant afterward. Of course, they didn't do it with me—they just kissed me and grabbed my tits. F--- It was scary then.'

Lola nodded. 'I remember it.'

'Do you Lol.' Paris blinked.

'Remember those guys at the Fifa Club?' Jasmin asked.

'Which guys?' Paris compressed her gaze.

'Those big-balled, rugby players from Sydney.'

'Yeah, I remember. That was fun, those rugby players chasing us, hooting in that big limo. They were in their twenties or thirties. It was three in the morning. That red-headed one kept saying from the window that he was famous, but that we didn't know him. And he was getting pissed off.' Paris deepened her voice: '"Come on babe, don't you know me? I own this limo. I got my manager here. He could organize something for us." I'm like nu! He was an ugly dude. A face smashed back like a dog run over by a truck. I wasn't going to f--- shit like that. And his friends were dogs, too.' Paris stuck her tongue out, and made a fart sound.

'They looked really angry, Paris,' Lola stated. 'I didn't feel comfortable.'

'You never feel comfortable.' Paris raised her lip and huffed. 'Anyway, they weren't interested in you. They were dicks on heat.'

'Yeah. I wish I was there that night to see these wankers.' Tony kicked the sand.

'I told them to go to the Emporium down Kings Street. They should meet girls right for them, those saggy arsed old hags. F--- were they pissed off when I said that. I was too cute for them. I don't care how famous people are. I can meet them through my dad, anyway.'

'Paris, they stopped the car and they were about to get out. The sight of the police car stopped them.' Lola checked Paris' face for a response.

'You remember boring stuff.' Jasmin interjected.

'If it wasn't for that cop car who knows what they could have done.'

'Yeah, who knows. Me and Jasmin were too good looking for them, so they drove off.'

'I don't think that's the reason they left.'

'I don't want to talk about this anymore. That's enough.' Paris cut the air with her hand.

'But you love the attention, don't you Paris?' Kua raised his face at Paris. He then looked at everyone to celebrate the claim. 'The worst thing for Paris is to be ignored.' He yo-yoed back to Paris. 'You loved it that those famous rugby players paid attention to you.'

'What!'

'You'd risk getting raped to make sure you're desirable.'

'What are you going on about?' Paris' voice became squeaky and high-pitched.

'You're a bitch.'

'Well.'

'You may be hot. But you're a bitch. You deserve to be gang-banged.'

'I don't f--- under conditions like them.'

'I reckon Paris is the one who likes to be in control here. Paris, everyone follows you. Don't you think she's the queen?' Kua looked at everyone, drink still in hand, as he slurred the words. 'Everyone here loves you Paris.'

The group watched on. 'I think the guys here would do it with you if they had the chance.'

'Don't talk like that, we've got a special code.' Paris smiled and fluttered her eyes.

The boys were staring at Paris for a moment and then pulled back that stare. Studying her seemed unusual. Paris was hardly ever questioned and the rules that Paris created were always followed without too much analysis. When it came down to it, no one really had a relationship with Paris, relating to her just meant following her.

Perhaps they were starting to entertain the thoughts they would usually keep under control. They drank beer and wavered. Paris sat playing with the sand.

'Go on, have your way with this one. That's what she wants. Give her what she wants.' Kua continued.

Paris found a stick and held onto it. 'F--- off mann. What are you going on about? Are you really for real?'

Tony sat next to Paris. Whatever ideas passed their minds disappeared with Paris' clarity-defining question, as it punctured through the beer haze.

'What's your problem? She's a tease, that's what she wants. With her manicured nails,' Kua acted like a girl showing his hands, and continued, 'her slim figure, the way she acts.' He held his waist and walked like a model. 'She's a tease. Give it to her.'

'No.' Paris was looking worried. 'I am not f--k--g anyone under these conditions.'

'Don't listen to her. Yes really means No. Right now. All of us on her.'

'Would you stop it!' Paris was staring at the dying flame, holding onto the stick.

'Look her insides are asking for it. Before she grabbed my cigarette. I knew what she meant.'

'Would you stop it! Stop it you bastard!'

Lola's heart sank. She looked at the dark desert and ran into it like it were a cave that could hide her. She could hear Kua's voice as she ran. 'Lola don't run away.'

Lola tripped over the stones and shrubs, as she tried to avoid Kua.

'Lola stop!'

'I don't want to see you again,' she cried.

'Listen to me Lola!' He grabbed her.

'Please, this is one of the worst days of my life. What are you going to do, rape me? And worse, you've just described Paris like you want her or something. F--- off!' She spat in his face as he bent next to her. Kua looked like he had a force within him to explain himself. He held onto her arms, and shook her. 'I did it for you! I said those things about her to teach her a lesson.'

'She looks head messed now.'

'She's a pretentious bitch. She thinks the sun shines out of her ass. Look ...' He paused. 'I don't believe in rape.' Alcohol was still strong on his breath. 'I don't think her male friends would have done that to her. If I thought they would've, I, I, I would never have provoked them.'

Lola calmed down. 'Were you trying to play a game again, like you did the first night I met you?'

'Yes.' He sat next to Lola. 'The abyss between me and your friends is huge. I've been with girls like Paris before to prove, prove something to myself, that I'm not just some dead ass … I don't know. People don't understand Aboriginals. They don't know us. I keep having to work at whites and their ilk. But I'm f--k-d up by this scene I'm in … I don't know man …' He let his forehead collapse into his hand.

'Like what? What scene?'

'Music. You know the music scene, what it's like. I'm not ready for a relationship.' Kua brought his head between his knees and flicked the sweat off.

'Do you just see me as a friend?' The thoughts about not being sexy and feeling ugly assailed her.

'I feel comfortable with you.'

Was this it? Was this the truth? He only felt comfortable with her? Lola held sand in her hand. The sand running through her fingers was like the relationship slipping away from her.

'Yes, that's it.'

'Why?'

'Because firstly I have never had a serious relationship with a white girl. I like to be true to my people and be with a black girl. If I slept with you, it would only be just that. I sense your melancholy and I don't want to distress you more.' It all came out of Kua. He was expended.

'I see.' A tear shed on her cheek, she was touched by the way he understood her.

'I'll be your friend.' Kua said

'Can you do me a favour?'

He nodded.

'Can you just show me what it's like to be bloody kissed. I've never been kissed in my life. It doesn't have to mean anything.'

'Are you sure?' He moved closer. Lola felt his full lips. Her mouth opened, instinctively. His tongue ferociously searched her mouth. He stopped. 'I got carried away.' He touched her shoulder. 'Let's walk back to the group.'

They walked back to where they left them, but there was no one left. Lola and Kua walked back to the house. Paris, Sam and Tony were inside. Paris was crying seated on the chair in the kitchen. Kua walked up to her, and bent down to her level. 'Look what I said before, I just did it to show you what you're about and how you appear to others. I don't believe in rape. But you are f--k--g arrogant.' The beer was still speaking.

'Leave me alone! Jasmin's missing.'

Kua looked around, Sam and Tony were tight-lipped and serious.

'Do you have any idea where Jasmin could be?' Kua asked.

'I don't know. She ran off. She was really pissed. She headed towards the left. We looked but we can't see her anywhere.' Tony started pacing a bit with his hands in his pockets. The grog was starting to wear off.

'We thought about calling the cops.' Sam stared at the ground.

'Let's check the water holes.' Kua walked out of the house. He grabbed a torchlight from the porch table. The others followed. But it was the case of the drunk looking for a drunk.

'Oh no! She couldn't be there?' Paris was crying. She kept wiping her nose with tissues from her make-up bag. 'Oh God!' Lola thought she should say something to console her, but didn't always know how to be herself with Paris.

The desert was looking very secretive. 'We've got to find her.' Paris stumbled over those words. She didn't know which direction to go in.

'When did she run off?' Kua asked. He grabbed his forehead, and bent over with pain. 'I gotta splitting headache.' He got up. 'This is too much.'

Tony arrested Kua's arm. 'She looked really upset throughout the time you were f-----g around with everyone's head. She left when you were talking like a shit head to Paris. Paz is her world. Paz gets hurt, she gets hurt.'

'I didn't want anyone to get hurt.'

They walked and walked and walked.

'Where are these water holes?' Lola forgot about her differences with Paris and Jasmin. After all, they were girls just like her. They were vulnerable, just like her. Suddenly, her problems with her body image stacked up as irrelevant. What mattered now was that Jasmin was alive. They called out Jasmin! Jasmin! They were met with the blaring cricket sounds. The desert looked seamless, endless. Kua was stumbling. The alcohol had not yet worn off him. They tumbled over each other trying to trace where the other one was going. There was the trickling sound of water. Kua flashed the site with a torchlight. Jasmin was slumped by the edge of the water hole. She had just managed to get out. They jostled over rocks to get to her.

'Is she alive?' Paris asked as Kua checked her neck for a pulse. One breast escaped its cleavage, pushed out by her Lycra dress. Her face pale, her hair wet and black in the night.

'I can't find a pulse. God, she feels cold.' He held her wrist. Kua's face looked tangled up. 'Hang on there's a small pulse. I'm going to try to revive her.' He maintained his head steady. He opened her mouth. He turned her head and cleared the water out of her mouth. He brought her head straight and placed his mouth on hers and began to breath into her. Then he pressed her sternum. It kind of looked sexual, but such an idea was ridiculous.

Paris brought her gaze to the ground. She was shivering. She looked very alone and so serious, she looked about ten years older. It wasn't working. Her body was not responding.

Lola froze. Was this death again? He continued the CPR, his drunken body flapping over hers. It all looked pointless. Jasmin's chest did swell a little. He placed his hand on her chest. 'She's breathing now.'

'Oh thank God!' Paris raised her head from her hands to view the scene.

Kua slapped her face gently. 'Come 'round Jasmin.' One moment was passed over for another moment. Life and death were just a door away from each other.

Jasmin opened her eyes. And she did really open her eyes. This may have been the last time she would get so blind.

Lola had to walk. Everything was different. Jasmin had changed, Paris had changed. No more shenanigans. Jasmin could not be the way she was before. She was taken to hospital in the town of Alice Springs. The doctor said she had brain injury. Her brain was deprived of oxygen long enough for it to be affected. The brain cells had begun to die in the water. Lucky she was able to get herself out of the water before she completely passed out. Any longer in the water and she would have been dead. She had a degree of hypnoxic, anoxic brain injuries. One thing for sure, Jasmin was no longer herself. And she was on anti-seizure drugs for a whole week. Paris couldn't deal with Jasmin. Paris and Jasmin must have really loved each other. They were great friends. They had always undermined their friendship by making it look like fluff. Emotions never really mattered.

Emotions did matter to Aboriginal people. Walkabout was important. It would clear the mind, connect you with a feeling that you're close to nature. Make you feel spiritually alive. It was a rite of passage for boys, before they'd become men. Lola used the idea for herself. So she kept walking. The hot sun did not matter. The weight of the heat was good. The gum trees, friends. The land alive, barren but alive. She was blitzed, in a meditative state, in a trance. She kept walking. Not afraid of getting lost … just blitzed by the sun, by the dry landscape, the empty horizon bejewelled by a few clouds. She edged near death. She felt her parents watch her. She was not alone. And as it got darker, as the sun sank back into its cradle, her skin cooled down. The heat dissipated. She went back to the house, of waiting …

Jasmin was out of hospital after a week. She needed to go back to Melbourne to commence physiotherapy. Jasmin nodded to what the doctor said, whatever advice she gave, with her eyes heavy, her movements slow.

The group went to Uluru. They needed a diversion. They needed to cheer up. They looked at the beautiful rock with shades of orange and purple. It was steady, they climbed it a bit and then a bit more. Jasmin walked slowly, only climbing a little and then going back down again. Jasmin, a seventeen-year-old girl, rested against the sacred rock speechless. She was lucky to be alive.

Lola refused to walk on the rock. It was sacrilegious to walk on the rock. Kua walked on the rock against the intentions of his tribe, the Anangu people.

Chapter Two

second chance

Lola and Alex weren't crazy about the two-bedroom flat in Richmond. Too expensive, over-rated. But that was the best you were going to get in the rental market. Lola had just turned eighteen and got a waitress job in a Generation X Goth nightclub called Ink. She figured they chose her for her dark looks. But the paler skin had turned dark. She did not regret her outback adventure. She missed Kua, but she had to move on. When she came back to Melbourne more change was needed. She had to move out of home. She had to grow up. It was the fizz that couldn't dissipate. She was going to be independent.

She met Alex. Alex was a Greek Australian. She met her at the same interview, and they were going to move in together. It happened quickly. Alex was down to earth. She was enrolled in sociology at La Trobe University. Lola, too, was enrolled in La Trobe. After summer holidays she commenced to study English Literature, Drama and Indigenous Studies.

Expression was important to her, because it was such an issue. She was fascinated by Indigenous cultures.

'I think we're going to have to take that flat Lola. We've looked everywhere, it's so hard.' Alex had a slight Greek accent that was warm on the ears. Lola's grandparents actually really liked Alex, and Alex eased the torturous journey they faced in letting go of Lola. Alex was dependable. Lola thought that Alex had a really healthy self-esteem. She didn't take shit from people, but remained friendly and polite. She was not stand-offish, but assertive. Alex was into retro style. She had a Brunswick Street look. Her parents were first born Australian. Kitschy seventies styles coloured the flat. It suited their pockets.

The flat was just off Victoria Street where the Vietnamese community bustled. They'd walk together down the street, do their grocery shopping, peppery, tangy smells permeating the pavement. They'd try to get through the tangle of people jostling for walking space. The summer sun washing down on Vic Street, and more people cramming down the narrow path spilt with cooking oil and cigarette butts. Slick drug deals done—hand covering other hand and object quickly out of sight. This was day time. At nighttime it was a different scene.

sex and the goth ... and ... what did really happen that night?

Ink was dark with purple lava lamps and grunge rock music swaying slowly into your spine. Nirvana's cords bristling from tight quiet to cathartic loudness. It was an elegant pit of vampires, shiny faced and awesome sitting around coffee tables. Ink floated into the night, in its black incandescence. Creamy hot and jarring music came from Nick Cave, at his best. Lola felt kind of more at home here. This was the sort of scene that smelt of refinement. Women were not hoey. It was a stylish place for people in their thirties, forties, and fifties. The parents of emos. Their lacy dress sense, a visual eloquence that spoke about 'attitude', and of nihilistic and romantic longings. Mind and body meeting in Goth 'haute couture'. For a few weeks she did the night shift. Then it was the day shift.

Lola got used to watching the passers-by, perfumed and accessorized. It was two days a week work, the days when she had no lecture attendance, and it helped with her confidence. One day a young guy walked in with a smoky atmosphere around him. He took a note pad from a brief case and wrote things down.

'Would you like a menu?'

'No thank you. But I could do with an old-fashioned cappuccino.' The boy had ornate eyes, well eye-lined, and his tone of voice was well-pronounced and clear. He looked up from a large black hat. His blue eyes shone brilliantly. 'Worked here long?'

'Three months. I'm part-time, I'm studying at La Trobe Uni.'

'What are you studying?' A smile clicked on.

'English Lit, Drama and Indigenous Studies.'

'Wow. Pretty good.' His whole face opened up.

Lola smiled. 'What do you do?'

'I study, just like you. I'm studying Visual Arts and Classical History at Melbourne Uni.'

'Oh, right.' Lola noticed customers coming in. 'I better go. See ya.'

Lola could see him through the corner of her eye as she wrote down orders. Then it was time to serve him his cappuccino. She made sure that the coffee was strong and the froth not too overwhelming.

'Your cappuccino.'

'Yes.'

'I'd imagine that you made it quite well.'

'Well, drink it first and then tell me.'

'Are you of Italian background?'

'Yes, how did you know?'

'You have a sense of knowing your cappuccino. And you look Italian.'

'Oh.'

He took a sip. 'Beautifully done.'

'Thank you.' She smiled.

He smiled. 'Mm. There's a lot of smiling here. Come and sit with me after you finish?'

'I finish around six.'

'I better order some food then. Cakes? Any good cakes?'

'Yes. We have mud chocolate, cherry delight with light cream inside the base, fruit lovers cake and caramel moose exponential.'

'The last one sounds interesting.'

'Caramel Moose Exponential,' she wrote down.

'I guess I'm ordering backwards. Later I might have dinner.' He had a feel inside his pockets. 'Let's see if I have enough money?' He took out thirty dollars. 'I'm just a poor student.' He smiled again and put the money back in. 'Mm, what's one to do?'

'Why don't you just meet me outside after work?'

'I would have to agree with you there.' He paused. 'So six outside here. But I still will enjoy that cake.'

So six it was. The black hat ornate boy waited outside Ink, just like he said.

'Are you English?'

'No for God sake, I'm Australian.'

'There's something English about you.'

'Well, I'm not into footy. It's not really my scene.'

'You sound like you like red wine more than beer.'

'I love red wine. I'm a Goth.' He raised his hand to her ear and whispered, 'but actually, I don't mind a beer.'

Lola laughed. 'What shall we do now?'

'Have fun? What else? Let's go to Fitzroy Gardens.'

'I've never walked with anyone with a black cape and a big black hat.'

'And heavy eye make-up.'

'Who's your inspiration for the eyes.'

'Boy George, of course.'

'Really. Is that true?'

'Well, sort of, I will pay allegiance to my fellow Goths, outside of pop stars. I won't name them just this very minute.'

'OK. You know. I forgot to ask you your name?'

'We got so lost with each other that, yes, we forgot to ask. My name is Cameron.'

'Mine's Lola.'

'That's a sexy name.'

'Really?'

'Haven't you heard of Stanley Kubric's film 'Lolita'.'

'No.'

'Anyway, it's got a name similar to yours.'

'Wow.'

'Now I'm getting a feeling here that you're a bit low in confidence, in-spite of all your smiles.'

'I'm getting better.'

They arrived at the park, the Shiva moon embalmed in a cloud, the sky soft and sitting lowly over the desolate street. The evening smelt of early autumn rain with that slight summery coating of humidity. As they walked in the park, the leaves crushed under them. Suddenly, the sky started performing a curtain act, with thick cumulonimbus clouds growing. The Shiva moon sinking further into its silver padding to wait the night.

'So what do Goths believe in?' Lola asked.

'We believe in an independent way of thinking. We don't conform to society.'

'Yes.'

'We celebrate what's quirky or taboo.'

'Sounds interesting.' Lola thought that she would do research about this on the Internet as soon as she got home.

'Have you heard of the Romantics?'

'Sort of.'

'We are kind of Dionysian. We believe in nature and the individual. We are not into anything too institutionalized. It is a European tradition to question things. It's Post-Enlightenment.'

'I'm not a Goth and you're talking to me.'

'No you're not … but I sense that you don't fit in anywhere.'

'How do you know? I'm always meeting these guys who tell me they think they know who I am.'

'Really.'

'This Aboriginal guy acted like he knew me and had a real connection with me.'

'What happened?'

'I went to Alice Springs … to his home.'

'Really … fascinating … and …?'

'He just wanted to be friends with me.'

'And you wanted more?'

'Well, I've never had a boyfriend before, guys avoid me like the plague.'

'That sucks. Do you think you send vibes to them—you know like, "I want to be left alone"?'

'I don't know, maybe I do. Maybe I'm just ugly. I don't know.'

'You're not ugly.' Cameron's eyes met Lola's and became really soft. 'Going back to the Aboriginal guy. Did he make out like he wanted to have a relationship with you or something like that …?'

'Yes. And then he said that he couldn't because I wasn't Aboriginal.'

'It shouldn't matter that you're not Aboriginal. Why's he making a big deal about it?'

'Some cultural thing ... He wants to be true to his roots.'

'Mmm.' Cameron placed his long forefinger on his bottom lip.

'Maybe he likes Paris, this friend I have. She's really gorgeous.'

'She's a white friend of yours?'

'She's Anglo-Australian.'

'Right.'

'Why is this Paris so gorgeous? What does she look like?'

'You know blonde, high cheekbones, slim, approached by a modeling company.'

'Sounds like a dog.' Cameron laughed.

'He said that he used to go out with girls like that, and he doesn't want to anymore.'

'He sounds like he's trying to figure himself out.'

'Yep,' Lola answered firmly.

'So are you waiting for this Aboriginal guy? What's his name?'

'Kua.'

'OK.'

'What about your love life? You haven't said anything.'

'I've never had a girlfriend.' As he said this he walked with confidence. Lola was impressed by his nonchalance.

'Really.'

'Does it seem odd to people?' Lola realized how conventional she was by asking such a question.

'I'm not fretting over it. Who cares what people think, anyway.'

'Yeah.'

'So what, I'm only twenty-one. How old are you?'

'Eighteen.'

Cameron rapped his tongue around his mouth. 'Are you still friends with Paris?'

'I've lost contact with her. I haven't even bumped into her at La Trobe. Things changed.'

'What do you mean?'

'There was an episode in Alice Springs. Something happened … It's a long story.'

'Sounds exciting. Tell.'

'Our friend Jasmin almost drowned in a water hole in Alice.'

'Gosh.'

'She was air-lifted to the hospital. Now she's got some brain damage.'

'That's terrible.' Cameron, by responding to all this, further humanized 'Goth'.

'I think she's getting bitch therapy, I mean speech therapy now. I feel sorry for her, even though she was a bitch to me at times.'

'Was that a Freudian slip? Maybe she deserved what happened?'

Lola didn't want to answer that. 'You know she was really good friends with Paris. Besties.' She crossed her fingers.

'How's the other bitch taking this?'

'I beg yours.'

Cameron cut into her story. 'Did those girls treat you well?'

'Not always. Paris has changed though.'

'For the better?'

'Yes and no. Paris is lost. She's completely lost. I bumped into Tony and he says that Paris doesn't want to go out anywhere. She's all serious and everything …'

'Change is good and it's good to be lost … it's more real.'

'She was a party girl.'

'And a mainstream fuckwit.'

'It's a bit mean?'

'No, it's the truth. Truth hurts. Anyway, this event has really affected everyone.'

'They all hate Kua, the Aboriginal guy I was talking about earlier. I lost contact with Kua.' Lola's eyes fogged. She wiped the tear with the long black sleeve that cupped around her hand. She shook her head. Her thoughts moved in different directions. 'I've lost contact with my grandmother. I can't phone her anymore. She's too emotional on the phone. I have to give her some space, to come to terms with me ... leaving home.'

'Wow, you've been through a lot.' Cameron stopped walking and held Lola's shoulder to help her string her story together. 'You said something about your friends hating Kua. How does that relate to what happened to Jasmin?'

'Kua was having a go at her about how up herself she is. His words were strong ... Paris was getting offended. Then Jasmin ran off. She was really pissed ... and because Kua was cutting Paris down.' Lola took a breather and continued. 'No one can break Paris. Maybe her father has. She's got big issues with her father.'

'It sounds like Days of Our Lives shit.'

'Yep.'

'And where are you now with all this?'

'I don't know ... A bit out of it without my friends. I feel pretty f--k-d.'

'It's OK to feel f--k-d. There's something wrong with you if you don't feel f--k-d. On that note. We are home.'

Lola viewed the Victorian house. 'Oh. I didn't know that I was walking to your place. I was so lost in the story …'

'You wanna come in?'

'Umm.'

'Don't worry I'm not going to jump you.' Cameron took the keys out of his silky pocket, and inserted them into the door, the lace around his wrist rode his hand accentuating the amethyst ring on his middle finger.

'Do you live by yourself?'

'No, I live with a nurse. She's not my girlfriend or anything … Anyway, I told you I didn't have one.'

The outback story was for now cast away by Lola. 'Do you rent?'

'Yep. Expensive. I work as a plumber part-time.'

He turned on the light, and a narrow hallway with oldish, eroding carpet with caramel and white stripes came into view. He turned on another light. There was a narrow lounge room buffed up with crimson pillows on a Chesterfield black sofa.

'Take a seat.'

Lola sat and rested against the pillow. 'Thanks.' The house had a dusty smell.

'Drink?'

'I'm not sure what.'

'Tea, coffee, wine, beer, joint, you know the lot.'

'Tea thanks.'

'I've got Lipton,' he said as he vanished into the hallway.

'That's fine.'

'Milk?' His voice echoed in the kitchen.

'Yes thanks.'

'Sugar?'

'No.'

'You're sweet enough as it is.'

'Oh thanks.' Lola blushed.

The kettle started boiling. It shook with that lingering old timely whistle. Cameron came in holding two cups, shoulders up. 'I'm having the same as you.' He sat opposite Lola. 'Tea's nice. I love tea.' He sipped.

'Yep.' Lola sipped in unison.

'Cappuccino's great, too. You make a great cappuccino by the way.'

'It's a miracle I do. I never thought I could make cappuccino.'

'Mm.' Cameron raised the corner of his lip, as if some new idea was whispered in his ear. 'I'll go there after I finish the tea.'

'What?'

'Don't worry.'

'Please tell me.'

'You might take it the wrong way.'

'What? The suspense is already killing me.'

Cameron drank up. 'Are you interested in learning what being a Goth's all about. You don't have to become a Goth or anything like that, just find out, that's all.'

'Yep. It sounds fascinating.'

'OK, that was the question I wanted to ask you. But not the main question.'

'OK.' A part of her wanted to stay and a part of her wasn't sure.

'Would you like to be my girlfriend?'

'Really.' Her voice shook. 'This is what you're asking?'

'Well. I do like you. And you must have thought that I liked you.' He frowned. 'Why are you looking so surprised?'

'I don't know, I just thought that maybe you just wanted to be friends with me.'

'I'd like to be your friend but also a bit more than that. How do you feel about it?'

'I think I need to think about it.'

'Yeah, cool. Think about it and let me know.'

'Yep,' Lola said stiffly.

'OK, so let's move onto another topic.'

'What other topic?' Lola burst out laughing. Cameron joined in.

'How was your day?'

'I've got another job.'

'Yep.'

'I'm a writer for the uni rag 'Shout'.'

'Good one.'

'I'm gonna do research into alternative cultures.'

'Like Goths?'

'Yep. You're just the right person to know.'

'And Aboriginal culture?'

Lola went silent. She gulped down the tea that was getting cold. 'I better go.'

'What about contacting you? Number?' Cameron held his palm out.

She took a pen out of her bag, and wrote her number on his pale hand.

Lola left the house with the thought of Kua at the back of her mind. So a relationship was being offered. She enjoyed the offer. She was going to catch the tram home and think about a relationship with Cameron, and what that would be like …

La Trobe Uni was buzzing with students in the Student Centre. She walked into the headquarters of 'Shout', proud that her writing submission was interesting enough for her to smack a job as a writer. Suddenly, she felt talented and important. It was only a few months ago that she had felt like a creepo, a dag, a dissatisfied kid. There was more to life than hanging out with skanky girls with no self-respect. It was the submission of her story of the outback that got her that job. She felt secretly guilty that she used the story to her advantage. And there was more to discover about herself and life, more spicy truths.

Her first journal report:

In a corner Street in Elsternwick on a cold day in autumn I had the privilege to meet a group of girls twelve to fifteen years old. They huddled near a transistor radio searching for jazz music. The transistor radio was suffering with the sound of static, the girls wore cardigans with big buttons. Allow me to let you in more. They wore long skirts and flat shoes. And Look at this: Their hair was long and limp vanquished by big hair pins.

Jim Carey bucked teeth and big glasses with ever thickening frames they had. They stared at me, their eyes widening behind lenses, like absolute spacey weirdos They shouted: 'We Are The Girls Who Wanna Be Nerds Club.' I prodded them with my reporter eye and discovered that these girls, all ten of them, were not hopeless or hapless, or for that matter drop dead dead beats, but they were alive, awake and full of bite. They showed me their nerdy interests. They loved comics like Charlie Brown and the Marx Brothers films, they loved watching Gone With The Wind, they loved reading tomes like To kill A Mocking Bird, A Catcher In the Rye. Who are these girls and why are they here?

I first spoke to Katy, the one with the biggest teeth. 'We don't want to tweet, only twits tweet,' she said with a lisp. 'We don't like computers, we are the nerds. We like it just the way grandma makes it. We like sensible shoes. But we're Feminist.'

'Are you always dressed like this?'

'As long as it's necessary for girls to stand up for themselves, against bitch girls who do what guys tell them to do.'

The girls who don't fit in have found a voice. It's cool to be uncool. It's okay to go mad. Girls who don't give into pressure from the outside become strong women like Joan of Arc (Joan of Arc was thought of as mad); Helen of Troy; Janis Joplin (strong female soul singer of the sixties).

You don't have to be constant eye-candy for a magazine, TV, the movies, the crazy Internet or a miniscule terror, a text message with a picture of you poking your tongue out ready for some fleshy act, that some guy took to show his salivating mates. The ones who are really free own a brain and a heart and are free of bitch city that props up dick city. The ones who are more than just a great ass are the ones who are remembered. Their tabloid presence beheld by an inner-essence. Marilyn Monroe was a beautiful blonde who died young because Norma Jean couldn't take being Marilyn Monroe anymore. She was smart and sensitive, a deep actress who played an audience, who kept them guessing at who she was. Her magnetism unfolding graciously, slipping into her velvety sexuality. Was she like a potato that could be held and eaten? No, there was more to her that met your linear vision, more to her than just a piece of meat you buy at the butcher's.

Nerd Girls City is the start of a revolutionary procedure. They don't eat the 'I hate my body' diet. I struggle with this diet now. Boy do I need thinking contortion. I wish I had met them earlier...

Later on that day Lola showed the piece of writing to Cameron.

'It's strong.'

'Do you think I'm saying something?'

'I think you're saying a lot. Anyway, why are you asking me, do you need my approval?'

'Sort of. Well, I just wanted to show you anyway …'

'You're helping girls, it's empowering. Now just overtake the media, Internet and throw this to them. Girls probably hate the way girls are treated.'

'Yeah. I love it. I love it, what you're saying.'

The lounge room had that doofy scent of time, a witch's hatch patch with a stew of ideas, new and old, cobwebbing into eternity. Everything seemed encapsulated in timeless Cameron. From where she was seated, Lola scanned the books that lived on the shelves: Jung, Alistair Crowley, Nietzsche, Goddess Energy, The Life of Symbols, and so forth. Lola felt lost in the room's world and its possibilities. The lack of central heating connected her to the cold, with autumn leaves patting the window like soft cat paws. Ruby colours blared from the oak tree in front of the house.

'You've changed Lola. I love your confidence!'

Lola was by the window zoning out to the blood coloured leaves. 'I feel guilty.'

'About what?'

'Jasmin.'

'It's not your fault what happened.'

'I've really lost contact with them, how can I find out how Jasmin is?'

'You needed to lose contact with them.' Cameron stepped up to Lola. He placed his hand around her waist. 'Turn around Lola.'

'What?' She turned to face him. Their eyes gripped.

'What's going on? You've been coming here for a few weeks now and nothing has happened.'

'I enjoy hanging out with you.'

'Is that it?' He held her waist and then went close to her lips. His eyes crashed near her. His tongue tried to go in. It felt uncomfortable. 'I don't do this often, I'm sorry.' He moved away.

'Are you a sexual vegan like I am?' Lola smiled and sat on the coach trying to be relaxed.

'That's funny Lol.' He reclined next to her.

'We'll try again.' Lola moved up. Lips touched again.

They laughed and melted into each other and just at that moment went into a lock that lasted a while. A feeling of complete warmth spread around Lola's body. She was at last sponging off pure desire. She accelerated on him, lying over him enjoying his lips, his tongue in liquid meltdown inside her mouth, and suddenly her mind was blown away, as he was moving his hand under her blouse. She grabbed his hair and her body shivered with pleasure. It was like she had always been on the brink of it. She shook. Her body let go.

She stared out. Her body had made its exclamation so quickly.

'Are you OK?'

'Yep.'

'Are you upset?'

'No. It's the Catholic in me, I guess.' She moved her hair from her face and got off him.

'Let me kiss you again Lola I can't get enough of this.' He pulled her towards him from her waist. She scrambled away, and sat up.

His mouth was still wet from the kiss, his hair mussed. He sat up. 'What just happened?' He rubbed his face.

'Nothing. I just don't want pressure on me to do it.'

'Look, what just happened, Lola, was beautiful, you don't have to spoil it by worrying about it.'

'I can't help it.' Lola crossed her arms and bent forwards looking at the ground, hiding her face.

'I'll come back another day.'

'If that's how you feel.'

'I'll see you then.' She got up.

He got up, too. She pecked him. 'Bye.' And zoomed off.

As she turned the corner she spotted him staring out by the frosty window, a forlorn face dishevelled with pleasure and confusion.

She didn't want to be mean, but she felt overwhelmed. The explosion that went through her body needed reflection. On the tram streaming along Victoria Parade, as the cloudy day flew by, each thought lingering like a shadow, the technicality that was sex seemed like an afterthought after what happened between her and Cameron. What pleasure was already in her palm. But 'doing it' seemed a bit different. Victoria Street was belting with rain at breakneck speed.

She found shelter underneath the grocery shop's awning, with a tangle of pedestrians going past her slamming for cover, running on the slippery slope of Richmond's little Asia. Drug deals quickly done with sleight of hand between a young Asian guy and a Caucasian one, the smell of Asian vegetables washing down into the gutter, and a woman walking past with a stroller covered at the front to protect the toddler—'pregnancy' Lola thought—Vic Street was just a mangle of life strewn from all sides. And Lola just stood there waiting for the rain to stop. 'Contraception.' The thoughts crept from the interstices of her being.

The next day La Trobe Uni was swarming with bodies, hunky dudes and suggestive women resting under the autumn sun around the Agora, inspired by the mood of Aphrodite, lingering in conversations, waiting for the next lecture, young romance flourishing. Lola wondered about the effect Nerd Girls City could have on her. How important its feminist message was. But Lola felt lost in the cave of her body, a different world, and from what she could see, its desires were at the suck straw of life. This made her kind of uncomfortable and happy at the same time. But what really worried her was that technicality 'doing it'. How did people get through it?

Someone prodded her back. She turned around. It was Paris. Paris angled her chin up. She was wearing her hair back, and a smidgen of make-up around her eyes. A hint of tiredness was in them.

'I didn't expect to see you.'

'I didn't expect to see you either.'

'How's everything?'

'OK. Jasmin's doing physiotherapy. Are you still in love with that prick?'

'I haven't seen him. I've got a boyfriend, sort of.'

'Get f--k-d! Really?'

'Yeah.'

'What's he like?'

'He's a Goth.'

'Mmm.'

'Is Jasmin alright? I've thought about her quite a few times.'

'I'm sure you have bitch.'

'I have … Stop it with the bitch word.'

'Why don't you go and see her at her home.' Paris placed her hand on her waist.

'I wanted to but I've lost contact with you all.'

'Well, that's what you wanted.'

'Is she OK?'

'She's starting to speak better because of physio.'

'Will she ... Will she ever fully recover?'

'Don't know.'

'Do you want my phone number?'

'OK.' Paris shrugged her shoulder.

Lola wrote it on scrap. She handed it over.

'Cool.' Paris grabbed it in an officious manner. 'Here's mine.' She wrote hers.

'What are you studying?' Lola guessed the answer, as she took the paper.

'Politics. I want to be my dad's opposition party. By the way, my parents are getting a divorce.'

'Oh, that's sad.'

'It's probably for the best.' Paris nodded her head casually.

'I don't live with my grandparents anymore.'

'Wow. That's a move. Are you still a wowser and a virgin?'

'Yes,' Lola said with a hint of pride.

'Well, not everything changes.' Paris smiled.

'Do you still go dancing?'

'No. Don't feel like it.' Paris looked at her mobile. 'I've got a class in five minutes. Call me … OK wowser?'

'OK. I want to see Jasmin. I really do.'

'I'm going there after class. I finish at about four pm. I can meet you here at the Agora.' Paris took a cigarette out of her jeans pocket and lit it, in an almost masculine way.

'I've got Indigenous Studies as my last class, but I finish at six.'

'It's up to you.'

'I'll skip it and see Jasmin.'

'Cool dude. I'll see you then.' Paris skidded off.

looking for jasmin

The house in Toorak with its picket fence, gracious garden—lush green and cropped—hid the disability inside the house. Lola's heart sank. Paris took a step up the porch and pressed the buzzer.

'Hi Paris. My goodness Lola. I haven't seen you for a while.' Jasmin's mother Jennifer had auburn hair and a pouty smile, a fresh face that resembled Jasmin's beauty and bloom. The bit of freckles around the nose was also Jasmin.

A light green carpet and a sweet scent greeted them. The lounge room unfolded with its contrasting dark green couches and rosy cushions. There was a large wooden dining table in front of the humungous glassed doorway showing off a comfy garden with short trees and lashings of lilies, jasmines and jardinieres.

Lola and Paris sat on the couch. It felt like camel.

'Some bikkies girls?' Jennifer held a tin of Rowntree biscuits.

'I'm fine,' Lola held her hand up. 'I wouldn't mind a cup of tea, actually.'

'I'll just go and put the kettle on, then …'

'It's so quiet here. It's a beautiful house,' Lola observed.

'It's no big deal. Yeah, sure it's beautiful. Jasmin's dad's a builder and carpenter he makes fine shit,' said Paris.

Jennifer came in with an earth-ware cup. 'Here you go Lola.'

Jennifer looked at Lola. 'Now I know what happened to Jasmin was not exactly anyone's fault. She got drunk that night. I knew that she liked drinking and refused to listen to my husband and me, but I'd like to know Lola who the hell were you associating with when this happened? I want to hear your version of the story.'

'Well. Paris appears really confident and because she appears like that, she can appear really arrogant at times.' Lola looked at Paris. 'Sorry Paris,' and she continued, 'and … Kua, my Aboriginal friend, was having a go at Paris that night because of that. He felt he was trying to teach her some kind of a lesson. While he was doing that Jasmin was blind drunk and became really affected by what he said, and she ran off.'

'Well, that's terrible doing that. Paris told me that he was ganging up on her, and getting the GUYS to gang up on her … egging them on to RAPE Paris, for goodness sakes. No good boy would say something like that. That is totally objectionable. Lola, you had no right taking my daughter and Paris to Alice Springs to live with these types of people.'

'I didn't take them to Alice Springs, they wanted to go there. Kua gave them the address.'

'What are you doing going to places like that? Alice Springs for Godsake? Your poor grandparents. What are you doing to them?'

'I don't live with them anymore.'

'Oh, that'll be right. They wouldn't have a bar of you after what you've done.'

'It's not like that Mrs Hucksley.'

'Oh, so you know better than me. A peep squeak teenager.'

'I don't understand why you're blaming me.'

'You kept them there. Paris told me that you've been the ring leader. What Lola does everybody else wants to do.'

'What do you mean?'

'Paris told me how you're the sneaky one with eyes behind your head. You know everything that's going on. You were jealous of Paris and Jasmin because they are better looking than you … and you set Kua up to belittle Paris and Jasmin.'

Lola couldn't stop nodding her head. 'I never did that.'

'These girls are innocent they just want to have a bit of fun. But you set it up with Kua to pick on them and make them suffer.'

'This is not true.'

Paris stood from the couch and spoke. 'Lola I don't think you really liked us that much. You must have said something to Kua to make him act like that.'

'I didn't say anything to him.'

'I don't believe you. I read your bloody outback adventure story. You get off on people's suffering.'

'No, I don't. Stop accusing me. You don't know the facts, you're just making them up.'

'Kua was our friend. You took him away from us and made us look like real bitches or something.'

'I came to see Jasmin.'

'Yeah, like you're really worried.'

'I am sorry if I've done something wrong by you. But I can't be blamed like this. Now I'd like to see Jasmin.'

'She's up in her room,' Jennifer said, 'and you can't see her.'

'I better leave then.' Lola walked off.

And slammed the door.

It was night time, night time was dark, just like she felt, and there was nothing left to be redeemed. On the tram, on the way home, looking out the window, night lights shimmering in the winter rain, she felt her mind churning over the events. She tried to sort out one big fat confusion sitting over her: Was she at all to blame for what happened to Jasmin? Did she influence Kua's behaviour that night?

Ring leader? Was all that made up? She wanted to go home and talk to Alex. No, she was now closer to Cameron. She was going to Cameron's place.

Getting off the tram, she had to run under the wail of rain, no umbrella, getting drenched in her own fit of tears. The Fitzroy trees looking dismally stark once the view of them coalesced in front of her eyes. They were silhouetted against a pearly sky. The sharp wind snapped at her cheeks, and all the weathers stung her like the knife she felt in her heart.

She knocked.

'F---!' Cameron was covered in a black silk robe, hair wet, towel around his neck. The heat from the electrical heater emitted warmth from the inside of the house. 'You've been crying!'

'I can't take what's going on.' Lola stepped in and rested her head on his shoulder. He then brought her closer to his body with an embrace.

'What happened?'

'I bumped into Paris,' she said against the beat of his heart.

'Oh that bitch did something?'

'Yep. I bumped into her at uni. I went with Paris to Jasmin's place to see how's she's doing. See how she is, and ...' Lola felt the tears coming, and pushed them back. She tried to catch her breath. Cameron stroked her shoulder, 'Sit down.'

'Anyway, Jasmin's better, and I was looking forward to seeing her. But Jasmin's mum and Paris have blamed me for what happened to Jasmin.'

'How can that be?'

'They said that I'm some kind of ring-leader and influenced Kua to attack Paris. Paris thinks that I've pushed Kua against her.'

'You know this is some guilt trip they want you to be on.'

'I don't know what to think.'

'Paris is bad news. By the way, you know we've got a female prime minister?'

'Julia Gillard.'

'Yep. Kevin Rudd was pushed out.'

'That happened really quickly. A woman did it.' Lola stared into space for a bit, thinking about how Julia Gillard was so different to Paris. A different type of Feminist.

'You're not going to see Paris again, are you?' Cameron sat next to her with his bare white knees turned towards her.

'I won't make any attempt to see her but I'll probably bump into her at uni.'

'Don't take anything she says on, she's manipulative.'

'I feel pretty bad about the whole incident.'

'Jasmin got herself drunk.'

'Yep that's true.' Lola left Cameron's side and sat next to the heater, hands out, tracing its warmth, its old grizzly appearance could be seen more distinctly. It started hissing with electrical fault.

'Now a few days ago you left,' Cameron sat next to her, 'what happened?'

Lola kissed his lips quickly. He kissed her back and they went into a lingering pash that warmed Lola into a slight frenzy. She moved away.

'Here I am enjoying myself and poor Jasmin is half brain-dead.'

Cameron stood. 'Are you going to constantly talk about this?'

'I'm sorry.'

'It looks unresolved. You need to do something to sort your head.'

'I think me and Paris should talk to Kua. He'll explain why he treated Paris the way he treated her that night. Only he knows what was going through his mind.'

'Maybe he doesn't remember. He was pretty drunk.'

'He must have known how he felt about Paris.'

'Do you know much about him?'

'He's an enigma.'

'You probably still like him, which is why I'm calling it quits with you.'

'Are you serious?'

'Yes, the whole thing is dragging on. You live too much in the past.'

'You've been really supportive.'

'But I'm human.'

'What about me becoming a Goth?'

'I think you're more of an Aboriginal. Why don't you follow your heart and go back to the outback. Go back to the dude.'

'Maybe I should … I don't know …'

'Good luck with it all.'

'You're letting me go? So quickly?' She looked down. 'Thanks for being a friend when I needed one.' She looked up. Cameron had just made a decision for her, and it sounded too right. Cameron, with his quicksilver intuition about the makings of the world, had tapped into the truth. She couldn't avoid it. 'What am I going to do now?'

Cameron brought his palm out. 'Talk to the hand.'

Cameron with his irony, and intensity ...

'I don't know what to say ... I'm sorry. One of these days I'll give you a call to see what you're up to. I like you. You're a nice person.' Lola began to walk towards the exit.

'It's the end baby. Oh, I guess you never were my baby. Be off with you then.'

'I'm sorry about the whole thing.'

'Sorry's a stupid word.' He closed the door on her face.

The day dragged its feet. Lola found it difficult to focus on uni work, and on the interview with Nerd Girl City. NGC would have been proud of having a female prime minister. What angle could she take on the interview?

Alex walked in and a rush of sunlight hit the dingy flat.

'Don't close the door, please. I like the sun.'

'It's cold Lol.'

'It's too dark in here.'

'How are things with you. I haven't caught you for ages.' Alex threw her car keys on the bench.

'Don't leave them there, you're always leaving them there. You might forget them.'

'But where can I put keys? There's no great place for keys, is there?'

'You've got to find your way with keys.'

'Are you referring to your life Lol? You seem melancholic today.' She put the keys in her wallet.

'I split with Cameron a few days ago.'

'Really. Can I ask you what happened?'

'I still have feelings for Kua. But I like Cameron. It just happened so quickly … how we split.' Lola closed the door. 'It is cold.'

'You don't know whether you're coming or going …'

'I know.' Lola lay on the carpet and stared at the ceiling for a moment.

'Have you heard from Kua?'

'No. His mother told me he moved out of home. I think he's somewhere in Alice Springs.' Lola sat up. 'His mother won't tell me where he is.'

'You're probably better off with Cameron.' Alex sat, and crossed her legs in an almost counsellor manner. 'Kua doesn't sound really there for you when you need him.'

'Cameron feels like he's second fiddle. I don't think he's going to take me back.'

'Why don't you try … maybe he wants you to beg?'

'I can't go back. I need to see Kua. Even though he's very confused about everything, who he is, I mean … I really do like him. I've tried not to miss him, but I do miss him. I don't feel like I'm really being true to myself if I don't go back to the bush, and try to find him … There's another reason, too.'

'What's that?' Alex's brown eyes looked stealthy.

'I bumped into Paris, and she's blamed me for what happened to Jasmin.'

'God, what is that woman doing?' There was a pause. 'She plays you like a puppet.'

'You're right. She does play me like a puppet. This can't continue. I know what to do to fix her up.'

'What?'

'I'll highlight for her what she's not good at, besides everything else that needs to be done.'

Lola had tried to contact Paris to ask her to go back to the outback. Paris showed a firm No, by her never speaking back into the phone whenever she heard Lola's voice pleading on the other end. It was a cut off.

Lola thought it wasn't true that Paris was not interested in getting the facts right. She thought Paris wanted to break the insides of her, to bring her into complete submission, like a cat wants from a mouse. Lola knew that Paris was wilful and steely in her revenge for what she believed Lola had done. And Paris wanted to blaspheme her goody-goody image of purity, and truth. Paris was going to bide her time.

Spring time. Lola bumped into Paris at uni. She had transmogrified into a 'hippy chic'.

'Hi.' Paris held a politics book.

'Are you talking to me?'

'Yeah, well not really. But you stand in front of me bitch.' Paris laughed in a grotesquely snappy, happy mood. 'How's your Goth?' Paris raised her nose.

'We are not together anymore.'

'Too bad.'

'What's happening with you?' Lola pointed to Paris' outfit of bangles, bandana, tattoos with cupid arrows on her wrists, and a teal coloured skirt that billowed delicately in the wind. Paris was an oxymoron: a spring fairy with the gravity of a crocodile.

Lola imagined the in-your-face Jasmin as a hippy chic following this new path. Her crazy red hair flaring out, she would have been a screaming Janis Joplin treating the world like it were her stage.

'How's Jasmin?'

'A bit better.'

'Have you been anywhere special?' Lola couldn't get her eyes off Paris.

'Rainbow Serpent Festival.'

'What's that?'

'It's a music festival with workshops, like Belly Dancing and Reiki, Singing Bowls and stuff … It was awesome!'

Lola was wondering if she was missing out on some maturing experience she should have had. 'I wish I knew about it.'

'It's too full on for you.'

'Who are you to say that?'

'You go figure who I'm seeing now.' Paris studied her toe.

'Like you're seeing someone, like you are in a relationship, a real one?'

'Yes a real one. I'm seeing Baba.'

'Who?'

'Baba Sol.'

'Wow. So what's this about?'

'He's a sexual healer.'

'Right.'

'I'm having tantric sex. He's like a shaman, he can change from mood to mood, from person to person, from animal to animal. He's real fluid.'

'Are you talking shit?'

'No.'

'You always have such special experiences, don't you?'

'You're jealous?'

'Na! Well, lucky you've met someone who lives in such a world—so Paris can never get bored. How old is he?'

'Forty-five.'

'Yep, right.' Lola clicked her tongue.

'He's hot, you ageist.'

'What's he doing with an eighteen-year-old? Be careful.'

'He's genuine. He is pure love.' Paris paused. 'And he's hot.'

'Are you trying to convince yourself of all this?'

'I don't need to listen to you. You don't know anything about Baba Sol, except for what I've told you, and I should not have told you, because you're sooo immature. So after so many phone calls to ask me to go and talk to Kua, have you managed to talk to him?'

'No, I haven't. So the guy's a bit hard to contact. I just got to go there, find him, and put an end to all this wondering. Are you ever going to come with me to Alice to hear what he has to say? Or are you so busy with pure light?'

'I can't be bothered with Kua or you.' Paris walked off and raised her arm. Then turned around, 'Besides what's an alcoholic gonna tell me? That's what he fricken is, you don't see me near alcohol anymore …'

One month later on a blaring hot day, Lola got a phone call from her grandmother.

'What is it Nonna?'

'Jasmin wants to talk to you.'

'Where's Jasmin?'

'Here. Right here,' Nonna said.

'Is she well?'

'I don't know.'

'I'm coming over.'

Jasmin was seated on the shiny vinyl couch. The surface of the polished floor reflecting her innocently expressed face. Her hair conveniently tied back to stave off the heat, her dress cotton and cool.

'Hello Jasmin. It's Lola.'

'Hi Lola,' Jasmin said in a sweet voice. 'I don't see you for long time.'

'No. How did you come here?'

'Caught the tram.' Jasmin had a definite slow speech that struck a heart string. 'I know my way around now.'

'Do you hate me?' Lola kneeled by her side.

'No. Don't hate anyone. Miss you. Paris came to visit me, but you don't. I wondered what happened to you?' Lola could feel emotion filling her, the kind of emotion that most teenagers would feel uncomfortable talking about, the emotion called pity.

Jasmin touched each word with her eyes. Different to the Jasmin Lola knew. Images of Jasmin blared, her hardy outrageous selves of the past coming in successions.

'Do you remember what happened to you?'

'Yes, I almost drowned. I'm getting better now. Been painting pictures of what happened.'

'I'd like to see your pictures Jasmin.'

'Where's the Aboriginal guy?'

'He's still in Alice Springs, I think.'

'Alice Springs. I had fun at Alice Springs. But then I almost drowned. He helped me the Aboriginal guy. I saw him breathing into me … when I woke up.'

'Jasmin can I get you a glass of water or something?'

'Yeah, glass of water. No more ees or beer hey?' She laughed.

Lola went into the kitchen and came out with a glass of water. 'Here you go.'

'Thank you.' Jasmin sipped the water. 'This room is very shiny and smells nice. I'd like to draw this room one day. Can I come here and draw it with you in it? I always liked your home.'

'Really, you never told me before that you liked my home.'

'I never thought about telling you. I wanted to tell, tell, sorry, um. I mean tell you but Paris wouldn't like it if I did because then Paris would think, umm, think ... I'm sorry. She would think I didn't like, like her anymore.'

'OK.'

'I don't know if I will get, get ...'

'Are you OK?'

'Get any better.'

'Jasmin do you want to lie down?'

'No, I think I better go home.'

'Do you know the way?'

'Yes. Yes. I live just two stops away, remember, remember?'

'OK Jasmin. Thank you for coming to visit me.' She hugged Jasmin.

Lola saw Jasmin a few more times after that day. If Jasmin had been semi-conscious during the time the neurons of her brain were changing, it helped in making her more real and connected. A sort of connection to people that can be scary … for most. Jasmin's voice trailed through details with a slowness shown in her jaded face, with a stillness in her movements and with a quickening of the breath. A needing for reassurance was evident, the child Jasmin had always been was now a ubiquitous presence soliciting mothering for every half-baked thought. There would be a pool of frustration surrounding her until she would burst into tears, and then an ocean of emotion would swell and trip over to a sublime awareness … about her own personality … where she would watch herself peacefully, before she would lapse again into the gentle unknowing, the quiet before the next breaker wave. It brought to Lola the question of what is real and important. Jasmin's state brought one to presence, to appreciate life, and friendship, too. This was a moment of Jasmin coming through.

Now Lola could walk with greater strength and nothing could stand in her way. Everything else was superfluous, and transparent when brought against Jasmin's sincerity.

Lola phoned Paris. Before Paris would hang up, she quickly stated, 'Jasmin came to visit me.'

'What?' Paris held her breath.

'She told me she missed me.'

'Do you think she knows what she's talking about?'

'She seems clear to me.'

'She's lost the plot.'

'I think she's pretty real.'

'She's got brain damage.'

'She's more than just a brain.'

'How do you know she's for real in anything she says?'

'She makes more sense now than before. Before she was a buffoon image of a tart mirroring you.'

'I beg yours.'

'She's more grounded … can't you see? She doesn't hate me Paris.'

'Well, you're deluded.'

'If you have any guts Paris, you come with me to Alice to get back into contact with Kua. You definitely need to talk to him. I am sick of this game, Paris.'

'Alright I'll come to see what he has to say …' Paris' smoker's voice cracked.

Chapter Three

rapture in the desert

Lola and Paris got off the Ghan train. The dry, dusty heat of Alice steadily roasted the air.

'So we're here. Thanks for coming with me …'

'Well, I'm over Kua and the Jasmin thing. I want this whole thing to be finished. It feels hotter than the first time we came here.' Paris stayed under the canopy of the train station. The scenery was dry and dusty, a sea of red, just red all over again. There was a cab near the train station.

Lola walked towards it. 'Come on Paris, come to the cab.'

'I hope this isn't a waste of time.' Paris walked up to the cab, and got in.

The house was the same. Steady, and feeling like a homestead, organically outback. Lola knocked on the door. It was Kua's father who opened it.

'Weren't you two here a while ago?'

'Is Kua here?' Lola asked.

'He's gone on a Walkabout.'

'Remember the accident with our friend Jasmin?' Lola asked.

'Yes, I remember. How is the girl?'

'She's getting better. But we need to talk to Kua about what happened.'

'I didn't know Kua had anything to do with her accident.' The man looked baffled.

'It's a long story.' Lola replied.

'Is he in some kind of trouble?'

'No, but we really need to talk to him.'

'He hasn't been living here for about a year. You kept ringing before. He wasn't here then, and he's not here now. Now he's gone for Walkabout. He needs to do what his own people do, not get caught up with your ways. You upset the boy.'

'Can you please tell us what direction he went in his Walkabout?'

'You have no survival skills. You are silly girls, go back home. Anyway, you don't have the right to interfere with his Walkabout.'

'I know … we're sorry. But this is really important …'

'I don't think you know what you're doing … What about this one?' He pointed at Paris. 'She doesn't say anything this year. Last year she said too much.'

'That's not a very nice thing to say … I am really too hot and tired for this …' Paris slid a look to Lola, and crossed her arms.

'It's about the accident, please … we just need some information from Kua.'

'Go to the right and you might find him. Keep walking right. I hope he sees you because I don't want you come running back here.' He shut the door.

'We better start walking then.' Lola tightened her backpack.

They walked without saying much. Then Paris put on more sunscreen, and drank some water from her flask. 'How in the world are we going to survive in the outback? This is ridiculous.'

'We go slowly. We rest. Hopefully we might find him soon.'

Paris looked out to the horizon. 'There's nothing but shrubs.'

'Think of what Jasmin has gone through. Her time in hospital, her rehabilitation. Think of the ordeal she has gone through, and perhaps that might give you some courage to go on with this.'

'Treat this as some f--k--g learning experience.'

'Yeah.' Lola moved on, sweat pouring from her face, the sunscreen just melting away. 'Let's put it another way. Think of the ordeal the Aboriginal people have gone through, all the suffering they have gone through, because of the White Invasion. That's a good reason to walk.'

'You're so earnest …'

'I thought you believed in goodness … so what's happening with Baba?'

'I am not with Baba anymore. He loved a few too many.'

'And what it hurts?'

'Yes it does! Don't pick on me. I don't like being picked on!'

'Ah! Now you know what it feels like. By the way, I didn't mean to pick on you. You just think I'm picking on you.'

Lola knew that going to the outback was not an easy thing to do. But take a risk, so what! And it was the spirit she was following, not white man's logic about the dangers of the outback, that was part of Paris' way of looking at it all.

They sat under a sparse gum tree for some shade. The sun's swelter was making them bleary-eyed. From her backpack Lola took out two small cans of corn and Smiths chips. She passed lunch to Paris. Paris took the food. Paris slowly flared her nostrils to take in the mild breeze venturing towards them. It was a breeze that was sinuous, tracing its way through the thick heat of the afternoon. It offered some relief.

Paris couldn't focus enough to open the bag of chips—she was worried that the bag would burst if she tried too hard to open it. Her hands were going flimsy with sweat.

'Here, I'll open it.' Lola took the bag from Paris and opened the bag quickly like she had opened her own. They started munching, and then dealt with the corn.

Lola went back to the earlier conversation they had, now that she felt comforted by the small snack.

'What happened to Baba Sol?'

Paris wouldn't answer the question. She thought for a while. 'He dug other chicks, so I split off.'

'I didn't think you were into relationships.'

'I thought he was different.'

'He is different, he's not into relationships.' Lola raised her voice.

'He's into relating, but not into relationships, Oh God, I can't be bothered thinking.' Paris dropped her head between her knees.

Paris lifted her head with a deadening glaze in her eyes. 'Do you still love Kua?'

'Yes.' Lola felt that she needed to be transparent out in the desert. The desert felt like it was a place where you had to be yourself. 'Do you like Kua?'

'I don't trust guys, I don't trust him.'

'Stop it with the spin talk generalizations. I can see you're the daughter of a politician.'

Paris laughed a bit, then went back to her sullen mood. 'F--- off.'

'We better get back to walking.' Lola stretched her arms.

'Oh Man, I just wanna go home. You're a f--k--g bitch for bringing me here.'

'You're a bitch, you've been such a bitch to me.'

'Don't f--- around with me.' Paris gritted her teeth. They started moving again. Lola thought that they were going to be talking, fighting and walking for most of this trip.

'I've met this older man.' Paris smirked.

'Another older man?' Lola thought for a moment that she sounded like a sister to Paris with familiar responses to familiar predicaments.

'He's fifty-eight. Man am I going to push that geezer around.'

'Who is he?'

'My father's friend. He's got a big crush on me. He's married and everything.'

'Jeez Paris are you OK?'

'I'm going to flirt with him real bad, and give him nothing.' Paris laughed. 'He's gonna love that.'

'Why do you get off on hurting people's feelings?'

'Marvin is a dickhead. He's a Marvin. What a dumb name.'

'You have the biggest Oedipal Complex.'

'Are you talking about Freud?'

'Yes, you have such a father fixation. You never got enough love from your father, did you?'

Paris looked and said nothing. Then a raise of the hand and quick slap on Lola's face.

'If you're going to get personal.' Paris held onto the straps of her backpack resting from the slap. 'I hate f--k--g everyone. I hate men, I hate women.'

Lola thought Paris needed to stay with the angry thoughts she must be carrying around all the time.

'Why do you hate people?'

'Shut up Lola.'

Lola was enjoying annoying Paris, but she also felt kind of sorry for her. Paris' cool image wasn't there anymore, and there were no men for her to express power over in her super flirty, slutty way. Lola thought that she had cornered

Paris, that Paris was too tired to be anything else but her resentful self.

'Where's this Kua?'

'I don't know Paris.'

Paris' hair was straggly, her face sweaty, she looked lumbered by the backpack. Her face naked without her facade of make-up.

'Why are you staring at me?'

'You look more authentic.'

'Oh … God.' Her voice chugged in its sepulchral timbre. Apparently her nightclub voice was her real voice. Lola felt like she had captured an elusive butterfly in the Never Never Land. Paris' inscrutability was weakening.

'Are there any footprints of this Kua?'

'You know I haven't seen any footprints,' Lola remarked.

'A great help you are?'

'Any day!' Lola laughed.

'You've got bloody sun stroke.'

'I guess I've got sun stroke,' Lola shouted into the land's vacuum.

They laughed. Then quiet fell. The sun's penumbra cast dirty light over the land. Time was running out.

'Let's sit down … he is nowhere in sight!' Paris stopped walking.

There was the horizon, sand swirling … amber colours in the sunset, and a moon in the haze between night and day.

'The moon's going in.' Lola reflected on something Cameron said about the moon becoming more introverted when it's getting thinner, and how it reflects the more introverted part of life. 'The moon looks so beautiful, so withdrawn as it empties out.'

'Do you think we'll die here?'

'I hope not.'

'We're not going to find him. He'll never take us back home, anyway.'

Lola took a flask from her backpack and took a sip of water fearing that she would finish her own water. She didn't want to depend on Paris' water. It would be a catastrophe. Paris was running out of water, too.

It was cooler in nighttime. Much cooler.

'Take your beacon out and shoot out for someone to come and find us.'

'No, I don't really want to. I wanna see Kua. It may not take that long to find him. We just keep walking to the right like his father said.'

'Forget about Kua. We are lost!'

'Maybe we're not lost, but we're just panicking. Be like the Aboriginals, be fine in the bush. Tomorrow's another day. We'll look for a water hole …' Lola couldn't help what she said. Her values were her values.

'We're not Abos, we can't be like them. You're mad.'

'You can learn from them. Kua taught me to look for water.'

'Give me that bag Lola!' Paris pulled the strap of Lola's backpack.

'No!'

'Give it to me you ugly bitch!'

'I don't like you Paris.'

'I know, you set Kua against me.'

'I didn't, that's what you made yourself believe.'

'Give me the beacon!'

'Leave me alone!' Lola pushed Paris down.

'I'm sick of your crush on Kua.'

'I didn't come here just because I have a crush on Kua, I came here to get the truth from him. And that night he just told you the truth about yourself, Paris. You're a scag. You give women a bad name. You treat yourself like a piece of meat, you make me sick.' Lola stopped, and breathed in and breathed out. Then continued: 'You don't even believe that Jasmin liked me. You had her under your control all this time. It's funny that someone has to go through like a brain make over to be able to live as herself without having to follow you all the time. If anybody caused her accident it was you. You're toxic, you made her a drunken slob.'

Lola moved away from Paris and sat down. She glimpsed at Paris. Paris was sitting, watching, not saying anything, and then: 'I wish I could kill you.'

Did Paris have a cutting knife inside her backpack? Lola felt she could no longer control what she was saying or doing or what Paris was saying or doing. And the same with Paris.

'Are you going to sleep well tonight?'

'Yes,' Lola answered.

Paris walked up to her. 'Give me the beacon!'

Paris grabbed hold of a bony stick Lola had sharpened earlier. 'I'm going to hit you if you don't give me the beacon.'

'I never brought a beacon. I don't believe in it!'

'Get it out!' Paris pointed the sharpened stick at her.

'Don't hurt me! You'll be on your own here!' Lola spoke rapidly.

'You give it to me right now.'

Lola passed her backpack over.

'Thank you. I don't have a death wish like you do, Lola.'

Paris pawed it. 'Where is it? ... Where is it? Nothing ... There isn't one. You're a loony!' Paris started hitting Lola with the stick. Lola raised her hand against the beating, scooped some space under it and made a run. More beating. Lola's body was stinging. Lola grabbed the stick and now the stick was wedged between them. Lola pulled it out from Paris' hands, and before Paris could re-take it, gave a blow to Paris' head thickly and astutely. Paris slid to the ground. Lola ran and grabbed the torchlight. Paris' forehead was covered with blood.

As could be seen under the moonlight, the sand cast a veil over Paris' body. Lola walked away … just walked away, her heart pounding only for LOLA. Her scars burning …

She lay down. 'Mama, Papa, Mama, Papa … Mama, Papa, Mama, Papa, Mama …' and fell asleep.

It scrawled over her, a blonde in a willowy white dress skirting the dunes like a butterfly, her eyes black orchids piercing through the nebulous dust, her long nails, like claws, mincing precision, but she was weighed down by the weeping chunk of meat on her forehead. It was creeping with maggots … Her talons widened in anger, so she gripped Lola's neck, and slashed through her tendons … blood spraying out … She laughed with her eyes, and the laughter in them finally bayoneted Lola's soul. Lola woke. A film of sand hid any life. Her throat felt ominously dry. The serpent of doubt began to rise to her head.

Paris, her ligaments starting to show, her hair mottled with sand particles, was lying under the Eucalyptus tree, as the leaves glistened in a menacing way in their uncanny brightness. They formed a preternatural halo around Paris' ghostly form. Dead? God no … Not this … What a thing to wake up to. Paris' tiffany neck trembled in the trickery of the morning light. Lola picked up Paris' wrist and checked for pulse. Paris woke upon touch. 'Bitch!' She gazed up searching for Lola's stance on matters like a wounded dog, eyes semi-closed and crusted. Paris' translucence was now enmeshed in the equalizing process of nature. Where beauty turns ugly. 'We're still here! … I'm so thirsty. Where are we going to find anything?' She asked the same questions like she had never fallen into a deep sleep, where she could forget them. She stared at Lola, half scared, half threatening. Then she prodded her forehead. She saw old blood on her finger, and witnessed her level of desirability in nature. 'How disgusting …' She shooed away the flies attracted to the arborescent sponge on her forehead.

'Paris we need to start walking.' Lola tried to find the energy to do the normal re-take of the situation. 'We need to find food, water, and Kua.'

'Lola why don't you just face it. We're going to die here. You'll be seeing your mum and dad soon, look on the bright side … Ouch my head hurts.'

'I don't need this sarcasm.'

'I have no energy. My lips are so dry, I don't care for what I'm saying.'

'I feel the same way. I have dry lips, too. I have no energy.'

'You've got hope. Something I don't have. What really happens to you after you die?' Paris stared out into nothing, the wind offering an eerie silence.

'I don't know. Perhaps a better place.'

'You're strong aren't you?'

'I have to be.'

'What's a party girl going to know.'

'You know a lot Paris.'

'What do I know?'

'There must be something inside you that you value and know.'

'Maybe I will know one day. Perhaps it's too late … My real name's not Paris, by the way.'

'What is it?'

'It's … Patricia,' Paris smirked. I changed it when I was a kid. Later on went to the Registry Office.'

'Would you ever take that name back?' Lola had just killed a witchery grub with the stick.

'No … I still like Paris. I thought I'd tell you a secret before I go.'

'Paris, please cheer up.' Lola studied her wound. 'Hold this leaf to your wound. It could stop it from getting an infection.'

'Yeah, right.' Paris staggered up holding the leaf. 'Thanks bitch. What's this paste thing on it?'

'It's witchery grub.'

'Oh yuck.' Paris flicked the paste off her forehead.

'Keep it on. Do what I say.'

'We should have brought Detol.'

Lola stabbed another witchery grub she had just found on the ghost gum. She squeezed it with her hands, and spread it on her own bruises.

'That looks gross.'

Lola took the coveted weapon, and started digging, then looked up. 'There's more ghost gums on the other side. Let's get over there. We're more likely to find water.'

Lola started digging again. No water was evident, yet.

'What use is this?'

'We have to keep trying.' Lola dug again. No water. No water. No water. No water. Again. 'Water!!'

'Yes.' Lola smiled up to the sky, like God was there, and went inside the cavern.

'I can't believe it!' Paris closed her eyes, and nodded her head.

They went inside the water and sucked it out from their hands. The water was luscious, and cold. It had been kept cool under the ground. It felt like a purification.

'If you dig in the right areas you can find water. Kua taught me that … You know Aboriginals taught lots of white dudes where to find water. Explorers would get their camels to drink gallons and gallons, leaving the Aboriginals with nothing. Shall we start walking and looking around?'

Paris smiled. 'You're doing well Lola.'

Lola smiled back. They climbed out of the land's cavernous gift.

The sun was a demon, with its eldritch carcasses able to be seen from far away.

Suddenly, a fast paced snake squirmed in front of them padding the sand, then going underneath it, only to dexterously emerge from it, and squirm over it again. 'That's the only food I see,' Lola said. 'We have to try and catch that one. It looks like a Carpet Python. They're not venomous.'

'We follow it, and kill it, then?' Paris asked.

'We have to kill it with respect. It's a snake, too, could represent the Rainbow Serpent. The Rainbow Serpent is subterranean … it moves in and up, and as you can see there is water under this land.'

'Did you hear that from Kua, too?'

'Yes … I need to pray, now.' She gathered momentum with the death-life lever balancing inside her grip, and recited the words in her mouth: 'Please, Snake give permission to die, and your sacrifice will be honoured as part of nature's death-life principle.' Lola never really did find out if there was an actual prayer, but she made one up herself she felt was close to what an actual one could be, if there was one. She knew that Aboriginal people felt an interconnectedness with everything, and hunting was part of that interconnectedness or Tjurka, as the Aboriginal people of the Red Centre called it, and when hunting, this should be kept in mind. Tjurka defines the flowing relationship between people, animals, and the land. One cannot exist without the other, the threads of life all coming together.

'Hurry up!'

The snake swivelled its gray and brown body, its fast 's' shapes, roller-coasting over the dunes. Lola threw the spear. The snake hid inside the sand ... And didn't come out.

'This is hopeless.' Paris stopped running and rested on the sand dune. 'We're going to die here, can't you see that? There's nothing in this God forsaken place.'

'Maybe I had a past life as an Aboriginal.' Lola stopped and stared out.

'You're mad! You're not even able to catch a snake.'

'You actually need better equipment than a sharpened stick. A woomera would have been great. That spearthrower has incredible speed, it's thin, light and acts as an extension of your arm.' Lola rested and picked up sand. 'The sand is so soft. We are lucky we're in this area of the desert. This sand for some reason is really silky here.'

'Aren't you afraid to kick the bucket?'

'I don't know. I don't know if I'm afraid. I'm not even sure if I feel hungry. I feel nothing, perhaps some inspiration.'

'You're f--k-d mann.'

'Maybe I'm not f--k-d. I've always been an outsider.' Lola's eyes steeled to the desert.

'You're just sitting there, just looking out like this is your place?'

'I've been thinking a lot for a while. There's a feeling of surrender in the desert.'

'A feeling of surrender.' Paris parroted the words. 'Have you been feeling this way now, or always?'

'Ever since I came to Alice Springs. I thought I'd surrender to something better, a better life, perhaps live here with Kua. And now ... maybe die here ...'

'So romantic.'

'No, it's real. This is reality for me, it's not romantic.'

'You don't belong anywhere, do you?'

'No.'

'You think you're better than everyone else. Lola I think you're arrogant. You think I'm arrogant?'

'You're definitely that.'

'I am arrogant. My arrogance I'll take to the grave. But why haven't you killed me?' Paris asked.

'You're a human being, aren't you?'

There was a low grade sound, building up from the distance. It was hi-cupping from under the ground.

'Did you hear that?' Lola asked.

'It sounds like animals.'

'Look!'

A profile of a row of camels had emerged about one kilometre away. There were people on them.

'Hey!' 'Hey! Stop!' 'Please Stop!'

'Hey! Look!' 'Look who's here!'

The men stopped their camels, and re-directed them. The Aboriginals were dressed in outback gear with Akubra hats. They had flasks jiggling from the sides of the camels.

Lola and Paris ran and weathered the sun's rays in mid desert away from the dappled sheltering offered by the gum trees. Lola hoped that Kua was one of those guys. As they came closer, they noticed the men smelt like beer. There were six guys, and one of them was Kua. Kua alighted from his camel; in the distance was the visage of his ass in sway, contouring the sand dunes as he got closer.

'Lola and Paris. I can't believe what I'm seeing, it's been like a year.' Kua definitely had beer on his breath. 'You two look really dried up, where are your hats mann?'

'We left them behind. I can't remember where?' Paris wiped her forehead.

'We didn't bring hats,' Lola contested.

'How long have you two been out here?'

'Maybe a week. I'm not sure. We just ran out of food and water. I found water today with the help of this stick.'

'Just like I told you.' Kua's eyes united with hers, acknowledging the past.

'You girls have some water, and food with us. You camp with us.'

'We don't have much of a choice, do we?' Paris raised her chin, the angry fire had returned to her.

'You're lucky you're alive,' Kua whispered to Paris as she struggled to get on one of the camels. He held her arm.

'I'm OK.' Paris narrowed her eyes to his face, while flies zig-zagged across her wound.

'That's a nasty sore you got there.'

With each step the camel took, Lola felt giddy, delirious … The day was shifting, and clouds were forming … The desert warped, its resolution met with the tobacco hue of the sky meeting the land. Lola caught sight of Paris. Her body looked blighted by sun, and wind, as she rested on the Aboriginal man's back. Lola felt stronger than Paris, able to ride the rides. A burning heady mixture of grog and male scent filled the journey. Camel rhythm and booze made the Aboriginals cheerful. It made Lola cheerful, too.

At night they stopped, and the temperature dropped quite

heavily. Kua played two sticks, and a flame was ignited. The fire's tongues reached out licking the night, breaching the desert's cold, clenched fist hold on life. Grog cans summoned the celebration of rest, as it wiped against the mouths of Aboriginal men. The stars swarmed over the desert, lightening up the sky, dreamscaping into the night. Kua brought back a few speared Bearded Dragons and cooked the blessed flesh in the flames. The food was passed around. The second meal of the day, the first had been bread, nuts and nauseating warm water. The lizards were soft-textured. Lola refused the grog, and so did Paris.

'Don't give em no grog.' Kua raised his eyes to the man who offered it.

'Why not? A bit won't harm em.'

'Desert and grog don't mix with em, I know.'

Lola suddenly felt Paris' eyes hammer into her. It snapped her out of her other-worldliness.

'Are you going to talk to Kua? We didn't come here for nothing …'

Lola licked the food from her fingers. 'Yes I will …'

Lola caught Kua's eyes. 'What is it Lola?' Kua smiled, intoxication singing in his soul.

'Don't you wanna know why we're here?' Lola asked.

'Because yu wish yu were Aboriginal?'

'Well … besides that … Do you remember Jasmin?'

'Of course I do?'

'You know, she's still recovering from brain damage.'

'That night was tragic.'

'Who's Jasmin?' Another Aboriginal guy looked at Kua.

'She's their friend. She almost drowned in a water hole … about a year ago.'

'Is she OK?' Kua asked.

'She's doing fine, no thanks to you.' Paris interjected.

'What's with that tone?'

'I didn't come here because I wanna be Aboriginal. I came here with Lola because I need to know if Lola pushed you against me? If it wasn't for you talking about rape that night, Jasmin would not have run away like she did. She's like my sister … By the way, why haven't you tended to my bloody injury on my forehead?'

'Jasmin had no sense of her own identity … Paris … she WORSHIPPED you,' said Kua. 'It was you who should have run away that night, not her. It's funny the way things turn out. She was like an extension of you.'

'I look ugly, don't I?'

'Maybe being ugly for a little while, might develop you in some way. Take a look in the mirror.' Kua grabbed a small mirror from inside his satchel.

'I already have a mirror. But I've chosen not to look.'

'You look interesting. Ugly sometimes is just plain interesting. Your vision is very limited.'

'I don't wanna see myself dying from an infection.'

'Get a hold of yourself.'

Lola looked up and caught site of the cream spill of stars. She put a blanket over herself, and listened in.

'Don't tell me you didn't see Jasmin's worship,' Kua continued.

'I saw it. But isn't it true that you hate me, and Lola made you hate me?'

'Lola didn't make me hate you. Lola showed me how you affected her. We, I mean, I was just trying to show you, how superior you felt.'

'Superior?'

'Up yur self … you're f--k--g up yur self.' Kua drank.

'What do you know about me Kua? I think you should take responsibility for what happened to Jasmin.'

'She's partly to blame. She chose to get pissed to oblivion … I'm partly to blame, I admit it. I want to see Jasmin. I want to see how she is. I'd like to make amends for her in anyway I can. Paris I never got over what happened to her that night. If I knew she was going to react that way she did I wouldn't have mentioned the rape topic. I know I was really blunt. How is she Paris? How is she really …?'

'She's getting better. She can speak now, and she can reason a bit more. She's not the same though.'

'I'd like to see her.'

'Why haven't you already?'

'Because, Paris, this past year I've been selfish. I've been trying to get my act together, trying to get hold of my Aboriginal identity.'

'And are you?'

'Yes I am. I was tired of being torn. But now I'm getting stronger. I can't be torn any more than I already have been … I'm ready to see Jasmin … Why did you come all the way to the desert Paris? That's a big thing for you.'

'I wanted you and Lola to feel responsible for what happened, then I realized that's not the only reason I came to the desert. At the back of my mind, I realized I had run out of options, I had run out of steam … and I decided to let go … in the desert … I'm only eighteen, but feel like I have lived every life. Perhaps here I'm at point zero. In subtle ways, I've let go …'

'That's what you get in the desert. You need some witchery grub patty for that beast on your head, you know.'

Paris laughed. 'I'm so tired. I just want to sleep now … You know I wasn't sure what you were going to say when we saw you, and I wasn't even really sure whose side you were really on … you've always been a bit of a mystery … and I don't really know what you want … but I have got to give you credit for being so gut-wrenchingly honest about everything.'

'That's me, Kua.'

Kua walked up to Lola. She was seated near the fire. 'Sit down with me ...' She studied him. 'Are you really on a Walkabout?'

'Not yet.'

'I didn't' think so.'

'Lately, my Spiritual Journey has been this spirit.' Kua pointed to the can of beer. 'This needs to change ... I thought about you,' he said.

'You did? You actually did ... Do you have an Aboriginal girlfriend now?'

'No girlfriend. Since I met you, there's been no one. I've learned things from you, Lola. You're strong and as real as they come. You're my role model ... in a funny kind of way.'

Lola rested back.

'You need to sleep Lola ... Lola. Lola, Lola, I see those scars on you. It's been rough. Lola sleep now ...,' he hummed, and kissed her bruises.

A breeze rushed up her neck. Lola woke. The eucalyptus leaves were rustling. The sky looked opal. The clouds smudging the sun as it rose. Everyone was asleep … She could hear the sound of water … crisp … nimble.

She walked away from camp. There was the water in an egg shaped ditch. She removed her dirt stained khaki shirt and cargo pants. She felt the vibrancy of her own nudity … and entered. The water sparkled. She dived in, and sliced the water in half. She rose from the other end, relief illuminating through her. The desert was now peppered with the scuffles of animals.

Kua appeared.

'I knew you would be here.' He removed his clothes.

'You're not wearing anything Kua.' Lola laughed.

'Neither are you …,' he smiled … white teeth, the whitest of white, contrasting his black skin. He went in.

He swam to Lola. His hands then went around her waist, he brought his mouth close to hers. She kissed him, and kissed him. Kua throbbed inside her naturally, smoothly, her breasts brushing against his wetness, she mastered the ripples moving inside her, and entered the realm of nature, always denied. She was free.

The water stayed in her mouth with the taste of Kua. This morning was splendid.

A White Swan. A Black Swan, two obelisks noble in the desert, under the sky, over the land, in the dry and in the wet; teeming inside the invisibility … the structure of the cosmos. Black Swan. White Swan. Now in the Dark Space, invincible and daring.

All is now ONE in the Dreaming.

Acknowledgements

Thank you to my family for their incredible patience while I tended to the creation of this work.

And thank you to Sabina Hopfer and Christopher Lappas for their great contribution to making this book possible.

About the Author

Marisa Rita Zammit was born in Melbourne Australia to Maltese and Greek Egyptian parents (and throw in Italian and Austrian, and Eastern European, too).

She started writing in the late 90s and hasn't really stopped since. While starting a family, she also started her Masters in Creative Media which she completed in 2010, majoring in Creative Writing. *Lola's Walkabout* was conceived at that time as part of the course.

Marisa has written numerous short stories, plays and poems. She has had two short stories and one poem published in *Secrets and Silence* and one short story and two poems in *Friction Fiction*. She has also been involved in the performing arts—writing and acting in comedy and cabaret, as well as acting in dramatic plays. She sings and plays music in her spare time.

Marisa enjoys writing about passionate characters, and the myriad of things that colour a world. She enjoys writing with a certain abandonment ... cutting through the lies ...

www.ingramcontent.com/pod-product-compliance
Lightning Source LLC
Chambersburg PA
CBHW020613300426
44113CB00007B/629